MIRABILIA DESCRIPTA

THE WONDERS OF THE EAST

MIRABILIA DESCRIPTA

THE WONDERS OF THE EAST

BY

FRIAR JORDANUS

OF THE ORDER OF PREACHERS AND BISHOP OF COLUMBUM IN INDIA THE GREATER,

(CIRCA 1330).

TRANSLATED FROM THE LATIN ORIGINAL, AS PUBLISHED AT PARIS IN 1839, IN THE RECUEIL DE VOYAGES ET DE MEMOIRES, OF THE SOCIETY OF GEOGRAPHY,

WITH THE ADDITION OF A COMMENTARY,

BY

COLONEL HENRY YULE, C.B., F.R.G.S.

GYAN

Published by

Gyan Publishing House
5, Ansari Road
Daryaganj, New Delhi-110002
Phone: 011-47034999, 9811692060
E-mail: books@gyanbooks.com

Distribution Network
gyanbooks.com
India, USA, Canada, UK, Australia, France

ISBN : 978-81-212-9824-7 (PB)
First Published, 1838

2nd Impression 2023

Printed at: Gyan Press, Delhi.

MIRABILIA DESCRIPTA THE WONDERS OF THE EAST
Author: FRIAR JORDANUS

MIRABILIA DESCRIPTA.

THE

WONDERS OF THE EAST,

BY

FRIAR JORDANUS,

OF THE ORDER OF PREACHERS AND BISHOP OF COLUMBUM IN INDIA THE GREATER,

(CIRCA 1330).

TRANSLATED FROM THE LATIN ORIGINAL, AS PUBLISHED AT PARIS IN 1839, IN THE RECUEIL DE VOYAGES ET DE MÉMOIRES, OF THE SOCIETY OF GEOGRAPHY,

WITH THE ADDITION OF A COMMENTARY,

BY

COLONEL HENRY YULE, C.B., F.R.G.S.,

LATE OF THE ROYAL ENGINEERS (BENGAL).

REPORT FOR 1863.

In issuing their Annual Report for 1863, being the sixteenth anniversary of the existence of the Hakluyt Society, the Council have pleasure in announcing that the number of members has not decreased, and that the funds continue to be in a prosperous condition.

Since the last General Meeting, the following volumes have been delivered to members :—

1. "The Life and Acts of Don Alonzo Henriquez de Guzman, containing a narrative of his adventures in Italy, Germany, Spain, the Balearic Isles, and South America, during the reign of Charles V, translated from a manuscript in the National Library of Madrid. By Clements R. Markham, Esq., F.S.A. With Notes and an Introduction.

2. "The Discoveries of the World, from the first original unto the year of our Lord 1555, by Antonio Galvano, Governor of Ternate; corrected, quoted, and published in English by Richard Hakluyt (1601)." Now reprinted, with the original Portuguese text, and edited by Rear-Admiral C. R. Drinkwater Bethune, C.B.

The following two works are in the hands of the printer, and will shortly be delivered to Members.

1. "Marvels described by Friar Jordanus of the Order

of Preachers, native of Severac, and Bishop of Columbum;" from a parchment manuscript of the fourteenth century, in Latin, the text of which has recently been translated and edited by Colonel H. Yule, C.B., F.R.G.S., late of H.M. Bengal Engineers.

2. "The Travels of Ludovico di Varthema in Syria, Arabia, Persia, India," etc., during the sixteenth century. Translated by J. Winter Jones, Esq., F.S.A., and edited, with Notes and an Introduction, by the Rev. George Percy Badger.

And the following works are in progress:—

1. "The Travels of Josafa Barbaro and Ambrogio Contarini in Tana and Persia." Translated from Ramusio by E. A. Roy, Esq., and edited by Major-General Sir Henry Rawlinson, K.C.B.

2. "The Travels of Pedro Cieza de Leon, from the Gulf of Darien to the city of La Plata, contained in his first part of the Chronicle of Peru, which treats of the boundaries and descriptions of provinces, founding of new cities, rites and customs of the Indians, and other strange things worthy to be known (Antwerp 1554)." Translated and edited, with Notes and an Introduction, by Clements R. Markham, Esq., F.S.A.

3. "The Discovery and Conquest of the Canary Islands by Bethencourt in 1402-25." Translated and edited by Captain J. G. Goodenough, R.N.

4. "The Voyage of Vasco de Gama round the Cape of Good Hope in 1497, now first translated from a contemporaneous manuscript, accompanied by other docu-

ments, forming a monograph of the life of De Gama." To be translated and edited by Richard Garnett, Esq., of the British Museum.

5. "The Three Voyages of Sir Martin Frobisher, with a selection from his letters now in the State Paper Office." Edited by Dr. Rae.

The following six Members retire from the Council :—

J. Barrow, Esq., F.R.S.
Beriah Botfield, Esq., M.P.
The Right Hon. Sir David Dundas, M.P.
T. Hodgkin, Esq., M.D.
Sir Erskine Perry.
Sir C. Wentworth Dilke, Bart.

Of this number, it is recommended that Sir David Dundas should become one of the Vice-Presidents, in the room of the late Marquis of Lansdowne, and that the three following should be re-elected :—

J. Barrow, Esq., F.R.S.
T. Hodgkin, Esq., M.D.
Sir Erskine Perry.

The names of the three following gentlemen are proposed for election :—

Sir Charles Nicholson, Bart.
Captain Cracroft, R.N.
William Stirling, Esq., M.P.

STATEMENT OF THE ACCOUNTS OF THE SOCIETY FOR THE YEAR 1862-63.

	£	s.	d.		£	s.	d
Balance at Bankers' at last Audit	314	17	11	Translating	11	0	0
Received by Bankers during the year	234	17	1	Mr. J. E. Richard, for Paper	19	10	0
Petty Cash in hand at last Audit.	0	0	0	Mr. Richards, for Printing	146	15	0
				Transcriptions	2	15	0
				Postage	0	9	0
				Gratuities to Agent's Foreman for two years	10	0	0
					190	9	0
				Present Balance at Bankers'	357	10	0
				Present Balance in Petty Cash ..	1	16	0
	£549	15	0		£549	15	0

Examined and Approved, June 29th, 1863.

CHAS. CANNON.
WILLIAM YOUNGER FLETCHER.

PETTY CASH ACCOUNT.

	£	s.	d.		£	s.	d.
Petty Cash in hand at last Audit ..	0	0	0	Postage, July to December 1862....	0	0	5
Received Jan. 23rd, 1863	5	0	0	Postage for Jan. to June 1863, calling Three Meetings	0	4	6
				Two Letters to India (to Asiatic Society of Bengal) and others	0	4	1
				MacDonagh, for transcribing (see receipted bill, No. 4)	2	15	0
					£3	4	0
				Balance in hand	1	16	0
	£5	0	0		£5	0	0

CLEMENTS R. MARKHAM,

June 29th, 1863.

LIST OF MEMBERS

OF

THE HAKLUYT SOCIETY.

Admiralty (The), 2 *copies*
Ainslie, Philip Barrington, Esq., St. Colme
All Souls College, Oxford
Allport, Franklin, Esq., 156, Leadenhall-st.
Alston, Lieut. A. H., H.M.S. *St. George*, Channel Squadron
Amsterdam, de Bibliothek van het Collegie Zeemanshoop.
Antiquaries, the Society of
Arlt, Mr., Moscow
Army and Navy Club, 13, St. James's-square.
Arrowsmith, John, Esq., Hereford-square, South Kensington
Ashton, J. Y., Esq., Liverpool
Asher, A., Berlin
Asiatic Society of Calcutta
Athenæum Club, The, Pall Mall
Athenæum Library, Boston, U.S.
Atkinson, F. R., Esq., Oak House, Pendleton, Manchester

Dr. Baikie
Bancroft, —, Esq.
Bank of England Library and Literary Association
Baring, Hon. Francis, M.P., 16, St. James's-square
Barlersque, C., Esq., Bordeaux
Barney, Charles Gorham, Esq., Richmond, Virginia
Barrow, J., Esq., F.R.S. F.S.A., 17, Hanover terrace, Regent's Park
Bathe, J. A., Esq., 49, Upper Charlotte-street, Fitzroy-square
Becher, Captain, R.N., 13, Dorset place, Dorset-square
Beck, Dr., New York State Library, Albany
Beke, Charles T., Esq., Phil. D., F.S.A., Bekesbourne, Canterbury
Belcher, Captain Sir Edward, C.B., R.N., Union Club, Trafalgar-square
Bell, Reverend Thomas, Berbice
Benzon, E. L. S., Esq., Sheffield
Berlin, The Royal Library of
Betencourt, Alonzo, Esq., Philadelphia
Bethune, Rear-Admiral C. R. Drinkwater, C.B., 4, Cromwell-road, Princes Gate
Bibliothèque Impériale, Paris
Biden, Captain
Birmingham Library (The)
Blackie, Dr. Walter G., Villafield, Glasgow
Bois, H., Esq., 110, Fenchurch-street
Bone, J. H. A., Esq., Cleveland, Ohio, U.S.
Booth, B. W., Esq., Manchester
Boston Athenæum, The
Boston Public Library, U.S.
Bowring, Sir John, LL.D.
Bradshaw, Lieut. Lawrence, Woolwich
Brevorst, J. C., Esq., New York
Brockhaus, F. A., Esq., Leipzig
Brodhead, J. R., Esq., New York
Broome, Major A.
Broughton, Lord, 42, Berkeley-square
Brown, George, Esq.
Brown, J. A., Esq., Newcastle-place, Clerkenwell
Brown, John Carter, Esq., Providence, Rhode Island
Brown, R., Esq., Sydney Mines, Cape Breton
Brown, W. H., Esq., Chester
Bruce, John, Esq., F.S.A., 5, Upper Gloucester-street, Dorset-square
Brussels, Royal Library of
Bunbury, E. H. Esq., 15, Jermyn-street

Cambridge University Library
Campbell, R. H. S., Esq., 5, Argyle-place, Regent-street
Campkin, Henry, Esq., F.S.A., Reform Club, Pall Mall
Canada, The Parliament Library
Cannon, Charles, Esq., British Museum
Carlton Club, Pall Mall
Chapman, Mr. John, Strand
Chapman, William, Esq., Richmond
Chauncey, Henry C., Esq., New York
Chichester, J. H. R., Esq., 49, Wimpole-street
Christie, Jonathan Henry, Esq., 9, Stanhope-street, Hyde-park-gardens
Churchill, Lord Alfred S., F.R.G.S., 16, Rutland Gate
Colledge, Dr., Lauriston House, Cheltenham
Collier, John Payne, Esq., F.S.A.
Colonial Office (The)
Congress, Library of the, United States
Cooper, Lieut.-Colonel E. H. 30, Hertford-street
Corney, B., Esq., M.R.S.L., Barnes-ter.

Costello, Dudley, Esq., 54, Acacia-road, St. John's Wood
Cotton, R. W., Esq., Barnstaple
Cracroft, Capt., R.N.
Cranstoun, G., Esq., Corehouse, Lanark
Crowninshield, F. B., Esq. (per Mr. Stevens)
Cunard, Edward, Esq., New York

Dalrymple, Arthur, Esq.
Dalton, J. Stuart, Esq., for the Liverpool Free Public Library
Deane, Charles, Esq., Boston, U.S.
Delepierre, O., Esq., 3, Howley-place, Maida-vale
Delft, Royal Academy of
Dilke, Sir C. Wentworth, Bart., 76, Sloane-street
Dilke, C. W., Esq., 76, Sloane-street
Drake, Samuel G., Esq., Boston, U. S.
Dry, Thos., Esq., 25, Lincoln's Inn Fields
Ducie, Earl, 30, Princes-gate
Dundas, Rt. Hon. Sir David, 13, King's Bench Walk, Temple
Dundas, George, Esq., 9, Charlotte-square, Edinburgh
Dundas, John, Esq., 25, St. Andrew's-square, Edinburgh
Duprat, M. B., Paris

Ecky, John H., Esq., Philadelphia
Ellice, Rt. Hon. Edward, M.P., 18, Arlington-street
Ellis, Sir Henry, K.H., F.R.S., 24, Bedford-square
Elphinstone, Lieutenant
Ely, Miss, Philadelphia
Emmet, Dr. Addis, New York

Flagg, Geo. W., Esq., Charleston, South Carolina
Fletcher, Wm. Younger, Esq., British Museum
Foley, Lord, 26, Grosvenor-square
Folsom, Hon. George, New York
Foote, John, Esq.
Force, Colonel Peter, Washington, U.S.
Foreign Office (The)
Forster, John, Esq., 46, Montague-square
Fox, General, 1, Addison-rd., Kensington
Francis, Charles John, Esq., 7, St. Paul's Grove, Canonbury
Frere, W. E., Esq.

Galignani, M., Paris
Garnett, Richard, Esq., British Museum
Gladdish, William, Esq., Gravesend
Glasgow College
Glendening, Robert, Esq., 5, Britain-st., Portsea
Grant & Farran, Messrs. 21, Ludgate-st
Gawler, Colonel, United Service Club
Grey, R. W., Esq., M.P., 47, Belgrave-square
Grylls, Rev. W., Exeter
Guild, G. F., Esq., Boston, U.S.
Guillaume, Mr., Chester-square
Guise, W. V., Esq., Elmore-ct., Gloucester
Gyldendohl, —, Copenhagen

Hale, J. H., Esq., Park-road, Stockwell-common
Harcourt, Egerton, Esq., Whitwell Park, York
Harker, Turner James, Esq., 10, Northampton Park, Islington
Hawkins, Edward, Esq., British Museum
Henderson, Dr., 6, Curzon-st., Mayfair
Herold, A. L., Rue Richelieu, 67, Paris
Hodgkin, Thomas, Esq., M.D., 35, Bedford-square
Hollond, R., Esq., 64 Cumberland-street
Holmes, James, Esq. 4, New Ormond-street, Foundling
Home Office (The)
Horner, Rev. J. S. H., Wells Park, Somersetshire
Howes, John, Esq., Chicago (per Messrs. Low)
Hull Subscription Library
Hunter, David, Esq., Blackness, Dundee

India Office, 20 *copies*

Jones, J. Winter, Esq., F.S.A., British Museum
Jones, W. Bence, Esq., Lisselan, co. Cork
Jukes, J. B., Esq., 51, Stephen's-green, Dublin

Kennedy, Robt. Lenox, Esq., New York
Knowles, John, Esq., 42, Moorgate-street

Lavradio, His Excellency the Count de, 12, Gloucester-place, Portman-square
Law, William, Esq., Treasury
L'Ecole Normale, Montreal
Leicester Permanent Library
Lenox, James, Esq., New York
Library of Congress, Washington
Little and Brown, Messrs., Boston, U.S.
Liverpool Free Public Library
Logan, A. J., Esq., Singapore
London Institution, Finsbury Circus

Lott, Capt. E. G., 159, Parliament-street, Liverpool
London Library, 12, St. James's-square
Lowe, Right Hon. Robert., M.P., 34, Lowndes-square
Loyes, Edw., Esq., 33, Paternoster-row
Lyceum Library, Hull

M'Calmont, Robt., Esq., 30, Eaton-square
Mackenzie, John W., Esq., Edinburgh
Macleay, Geo., Esq., Brownhills, New South Wales
Macready, W. C., Esq., Sherborne House, Dorset
Madan, Capt. Frederick, H.C.S., 5, Northwick-terrace, St. John's Wood
Madras Literary Society
Major, R. H., Esq., F.S.A., British Museum
Malcolm, W. Elphinstone, Esq., Burnfoot, Langholm, Carlisle
Mantell, Walter, Esq., New Zealand
Markham, Clements R., Esq., 21, Eccleston-square
Marlborough, His Grace the Duke of, Blenheim
Marsh, Hon. George P., Constantinople
Massie, Admiral T. L., R.N., Chester
Melbourne, Public Library of, per Mr. Guillaume
Muller, F., Esq., Amsterdam
Munich Royal Library
Murchison, Sir Roderick Impey, F.R.S. &c., 16, Belgrave-square
Murphy, Hon. C. H., Brooklyn, New York
Murray, John, Esq., Albemarle-street

Newcastle-upon-Tyne Literary and Scientific Institute
Newman, Mr. James, 13, York place, Kentish Town
New York Mercantile Library
Nicholson, Sir C. D. E. L.
Nimmo, Thomas, Esq., Demerara
Norris, Edwin, Esq., Sec. Asiatic Society, 5, New Burlington-street
Norton, C. B., Esq., New York

Oriental Club, Hanover-square
Osborn, Capt. Sherard, R.N., 14, Chapel-street, Belgrave-square
Ouvry, F., Esq., F.S.A., 66, Lincoln's Inn Fields

Page, Mr. Thos., 173, North-st., Brighton
Paine, W. Dunkley, Esq., Cockshutt Hill, Reigate
Parliament Library, Toronto
Parry, Sir Erskine, M.P., Eaton place
Peacock, Geo., Esq., Starcross, nr. Exeter
Peacock, Septimus, Esq., Alexandria
Pemberton, Mrs.
Pennington, John, Esq., Philadelphia
Pennsylvania, Historical Society of
Perry, Sir Erskine, M.P., Eaton-place
Petit, Rev. J. Louis, the Uplands, Shiffnal
Petit, Miss
Phillimore, Charles B., Esq., 25, Upper Berkeley-street
Platt, T. Clayton, Esq., Philadelphia
Plowden, W. H. Chicheley, Esq., F.R.S.
Portland, His Grace the Duke of
Portsmouth, the Royal Naval College
Pourtales, Count Albert, Berlin
Powis, Earl of, 45, Berkeley-square
Prescott, Admiral Sir Henry, K.C.B., Senior United Service Club
Putnam, G. R., Esq., New York

Quaritch, Mr., 15, Piccadilly

Rawlinson, Major-General Sir H., K.C.B., Athenæum Club
Reed, F. J. Esq., 34, Bedford-square
Richard, John E., Esq., Wandsworth, Surrey
Richards, Thomas, Esq., 12, Addison-crescent, Kensington
Richardson, Sir John, M.D., F.R.S., Grasmere, Westmorland
Richardson, Ralph, Esq., Cranford, Exmouth
Riggs, G. W., Esq., Washington, U.S.
Robinson, Capt. Walter F., R.N., F.R.G.S., Junior United Service Club
Royal Geographical Society, 3, Waterloo-place
Royal Library, Stockholm
Royal Society, Burlington House
Roys, Thos. Wm., Esq., Southampton, Long Island, New York
Rowsell, E. P., Esq., 29, Finsbury-circus
Rumbold, T. H., Esq., 1, Eccleston-square
Rushout, Miss, Tetbury, 26, Onslow-square, Brompton
Rye, W. B., Esq., British Museum

Scarth, J., Esq., Canton
Schomburgk, Sir Robert, Bangkok
Sedgwick, the Rev. Adam, Woodwardian Professor, Cambridge
Sheffield, Earl of, 20, Portland-place
Shrewsbury, Earl of
Simpson, Lieutenant
Singapore Library
Smith, Edmund, Esq., Hull
Smith, George, Esq., 21, Russell-square

Smith, J., Esq., 5, Cavendish-square
Somers, Earl, 33, Princes-gate, Hyde Park
Sotheby, Mrs., Kingston
Stanford, Mr. E., Charing-cross
Stanley of Alderley, Lord, Dover-street
Stanley, Hon. Henry E. J.
St. Andrew's University
St. David's, the Right Rev. the Lord Bishop of, Abergwili, Carmarthenshire
St. Petersburg, Imperial Library of
Stevens, H., Esq., Boston, United States
Stirling, Wm., Esq., of Keir, 128, Park-st.
Stockholm, Royal Library of (per Messrs. Longman and Co.)
Stuart, Alexander, Esq., New York
Stuart, R. L., Esq., New York
Stubbs, Commander, R.N.

Taunton, Lord, 27, Belgrave-square
Ternaux-Compans, Mons. H., Paris
Thompson, Thos., Esq., Solicitor, Hull
Thomas, W. A., Esq., 50, Threadneedle-street
Tolstoy, George, Esq., St. Petersburgh
Toronto University
Trade, the Board of, Whitehall
Travellers' Club, 106, Pall Mall
Trinity House, Tower Hill

Union Society, Oxford
United Service Institution, Scotland-yard
Upham & Beet, Messrs. 46, New Bond-st.

Victoria Library and Reading Rooms, Hong Kong
Vienna Imperial Library
Virginia State Library
Vivian, Geo., Esq., 11, Upper Grosvenor-street

Van Rÿckevorsel, H., Consul de Venezuela, Conseiller à la Régence de Rotterdam

Waite, Henry, Esq., 68, Old Broad street
Wales, George Washington, Boston, U.S.
Walker, J., Esq., 31, Keppel-street
Walker, Joshua, Esq., Jun., 59, Upper Brunswick-place, Brighton
Waters, J. S., Esq., Baltimore, U.S.
Watts, Thomas, Esq., British Museum
Weir, William, Esq., 30, Great Coram-st.
Wensleydale, the Rt. Hon. Lord, 56, Park-street, Grosvenor-square
Whewell, the Rev. W., D.D., Master of Trinity College, Cambridge
White, R., Esq., Cowes, Isle of Wight
Whiteman, J. C., Esq., Theydon Grove, Epping
Wilkinson, John, Esq., 3, Wellington-st., Strand
Willis and Sotheran, Messrs., Strand
Williams, T., Esq., Northumberland-house, Strand
Wilson, Edward S., Esq., Hull
Wolff, H. Drummond, Esq., Secretary to the Lord High Commissioner of the Ionian Islands, Corfu.
Woodd, Basil T., Esq., Conyngham Hall, Naresborough
Wood, Lieutenant John, H.E.I.C.S., 137, Leadenhall-street
Woods, Samuel, Esq., Australia
Wright, H., Esq., Cheltenham
Wyld, James, Esq., Strand

Young, Capt. Allen, Riversdale, Twickenham
Young, G. F., Esq., 80, Cornhill

Rules for the Delivery of the Society's Volumes.

I. The Society's productions will be delivered without any charge, within three miles of the General Post Office.

II. They will be forwarded to any place beyond that limit, the Society paying the cost of booking, but not of carriage; nor will it be answerable in this case for any loss or damage.

III. They will be delivered by the Society's agent, Mr. Thomas Richards, 37, Great Queen Street, Lincoln's Inn Fields, to persons having written authority of subscribers to receive them.

IV. They will be sent to the Society's correspondents or agents in the principal towns throughout the kingdom; and care shall be taken that the charge for carriage be as moderate as possible.

RICHARDS, PRINTER, 37, GREAT QUEEN STREET.

WORKS ISSUED BY

The Hakluyt Society.

THE WONDERS OF THE EAST,

BY

FRIAR JORDANUS.

M.DCCC.LXIII.

MIRABILIA DESCRIPTA.

THE

WONDERS OF THE EAST,

BY

FRIAR JORDANUS,

OF THE ORDER OF PREACHERS AND BISHOP OF COLUMBUM
IN INDIA THE GREATER,

(CIRCA 1330).

TRANSLATED FROM THE LATIN ORIGINAL,

AS PUBLISHED AT PARIS IN 1839, IN THE RECUEIL DE VOYAGES
ET DE MÉMOIRES, OF THE SOCIETY OF GEOGRAPHY,

WITH THE ADDITION OF A COMMENTARY,

BY

COLONEL HENRY YULE, C.B., F.R.G.S.,

LATE OF THE ROYAL ENGINEERS (BENGAL).

LONDON:
PRINTED FOR THE HAKLUYT SOCIETY.

M.DCCC.LXIII.

THE HAKLUYT SOCIETY.

DEDICATION.

TO

HIS EXCELLENCY

SIR H. B. E. FRERE, K.C.B.,

GOVERNOR OF BOMBAY.

Dear Sir Bartle Frere,

There is no time to ask your assent to this dedication. But I have trust enough in your love for old travellers, and in your good-will to the editor, to venture it without permission. I have some hope too that I introduce to you a new acquaintance in the Bishop of Columbum, whose book seems little known.

Like many other old travellers of more fame, whilst endeavouring to speak only truth of what he has seen, Jordanus retails fables enough from hearsay. What he did see in his travels was so marvellous to him, that he was quite ready to accept what was told him of regions more remote from Christendom, when it seemed but in reasonable proportion more marvellous. If there were cats with wings in Malabar, as he had seen,[1] why should there not be people with dogs' heads in the Islands of the Ocean ?[2] If black men cut off their own heads before their gods at Columbum,[3] why should not "white and fat men" be purchased as delectable food in Java ?[4] If there were rats nearly as big as foxes in India Major,[5] why should there not be rocs that could fly away with elephants in India Tertia ?[6]

Apart from this credulity, it might be well if the heads of some of our modern sojourners in India could be endowed with a little more of that Organ of Wonder which gave these old story-tellers such a thorough enjoyment of the real marvels of the East, and could by its help see something worthier there than a howling wilderness, affording no consolation but that silver fruit, which, like the coco-nut described by our author, is borne twelve times in the year.[7]

Were Jordanus to come to life again, he would see many changes no doubt, but he would still find many landmarks standing after the five and a half centuries. To say nothing of the "Coquodriles"[8] and the horrible heat,[9] he would find the Parsis still disposing of their dead in their strange old fashion,[10] the Nairs still handing down their succession in oblique descent,[11] the Dóms still feeding on offal and doing the basest drudgeries,[12] the poor Poliars still dwell-

[1] See p. 29.
[2] ,, p. 44.
[3] ,, p. 33.
[4] ,, p. 31.
[5] See p. 29.
[6] ,, p. 42.
[7] ,, p. 16.
[8] ,, p. 19.
[9] See p. 22.
[10] ,, p. 21.
[11] ,, p. 32.
[12] ,, p. 21.

ing in dens and howling by the wayside,[1] the ox still "honoured like a father,"[2] and the idols still "dragged through the land like the Virgin at Rogation-tides;"[3] he might even hear now and then of "living women taking their places on the fire and dying with their dead."[4] Much therefore of evil he would find very persistent. How on the other side? He would indeed also find the Hindus still "clean in feeding," but would he still pronounce them to be "true in speech and eminent in justice?"[5] Is it not to be feared that he would find not only the wealth of that Columbum, which in the days of his bishopric was hidden by the masts of all the East from Yemen to Cathay, as far gone by as the splendours of the kings of Telinga and Narsinga, but the natural life and genius of the people degenerate and their inborn arts in decay? He would indeed see vigorous efforts in action to introduce a new life into the country; instead of Diabolus roaring in the woods by night[6] he might hear the scream of the locomotive; and he would meet among those Western conquerors who, in strange fulfilment of the prophecies of his own day,[7] are now ruling India, some confident believers in the renovation of the land through the introduction of the material progress of Europe.

Will that belief be justified? I am not likely to undervalue the work in which my best years have

[1] See p. 35.
[2] ,, p. 25.
[3] ,, p. 33.
[4] See p. 21.
[5] ,, p. 22
[6] ,, p. 37.
[7] ,, p. 30.

been spent; but surely that alone will not serve. The question that carried Jordanus to the East five hundred and forty years ago is still the great question for India, however Providence may solve it. Till India becomes Christian there is no hope of real life and renovation. Would Jordanus Redivivus discern much progress in this direction since the days of his episcopate? How like his talk about the matter is to that of our own missionaries in the nineteenth century![1] Hindu Christians are still a feeble and scattered folk,[2] and the advance towards Christian light seems to all who care not, and to many who do care, almost nothing. But it is encouraging to know that you think very differently, and few indeed have had at once your capacity and your opportunity for a just judgment.

I am ever, dear Sir Bartle,

Your faithful friend and servant,

H. YULE.

Genoa, October 14th, 1863.

[1] See p. 55. [2] See p. 23.

CONTENTS.

PREFACE.

CHAPTER I.

[THE MEDITERRANEAN.]

CHAPTER II.

CONCERNING ARMENIA.

CHAPTER III.

CONCERNING THE REALM OF PERSIA.

CHAPTER IV.

CONCERNING INDIA THE LESS.

CHAPTER V.

CONCERNING INDIA THE GREATER.

CHAPTER VI.

CONCERNING INDIA TERTIA (S. E. AFRICA)

CHAPTER XIV.

CONCERNING THE DISTANCES OF COUNTRIES.

CHAPTER XV.

CONCERNING THE ISLAND OF CHIOS.

CHAPTER XVI.

CONCERNING TURKEY.

PREFACE.

THE little work here presented was printed in the original Latin at Paris in 1839, under the editorship of M. Coquebert-Montbret, in the *Recueil de Voyages et de Mémoires, publié par la Société de Géographie*, vol. iv.

I cannot find that it has ever been published or translated in England, or even noticed in any English book, except in the *Ceylon* of Sir James Emerson Tennent, where there is an allusion to it.

The book itself does not add anything to our knowledge; but the observations of a traveller who resided in India so far back as the beginning of the fourteenth century must be very dull indeed if sufficient interest cannot be derived from their date to make them acceptable. Nor do I think our author *is* dull, whilst I regret that he is so brief, and has omitted so much that he might really have laid up as an addition to our knowledge. The very fact that there were Roman Catholic missionaries and a bishop in India at that period, just between the days of Marco Polo and those of Ibn Batuta, may indeed be excavated from old ecclesiastical chronicles; but it is certainly unfamiliar to the knowledge of those who do not dig in such mines.

The translation which follows has been made, and the brief particulars which I shall give respecting the author have been derived, from the *Recueil* above indicated.[1]

The manuscript from which the French editor transcribed belonged to the Baron Walckenaer. It is on parchment, of the fourteenth century, and contains other matter, the work of Jordanus occupying twenty-nine quarto pages.

The author is termed a native of Séverac. That he was a Frenchman will appear from several passages in his book. But there are at least five places of the name of Severac in France. Three of these are in the district of Rouergue, in the department of the Aveyron (near the eastern boundary of the old province of Guyenne, and some ninety miles N.E. of Toulouse), and it was probably from one of these that he came. There was a noble family of this province called De Séverac, of which was Amaulry de Séverac, Marshal of France in the time of Charles VII. But, as will afterwards appear, our traveller was called *Catalani*.[2]

[1] I have to regret that unavoidable circumstances have interrupted my pleasant task, and have compelled me to leave this preface, and some part of the commentary, in a cruder state than I should have allowed, had time permitted of the search for further particulars or illustrations of the author's life, mission, and descriptions.

[2] The French editor regards this as his surname. Is it not more probably only the genitive of his father's name?

The dates of his birth, his death, or his first going to the East, are undetermined. But it is ascertained that he was in the East in 1321-1323, that he returned to Europe, and started again for India, in or soon after 1330. There appears to be nothing to determine whether this book of *Mirabilia* was written on his first, or on a subsequent, return to Europe.

The authorities for the dates just given are the following:—

Two letters from Jordanus are found in a MS. in the national library at Paris (in 1839,—Bibliothèque du Roi—MS. No. 5,006, p. 182), entitled *Liber de œtatibus*, etc. The first of these is dated from Caga,[1] 12th October, 1321. It is addressed to members of his own order (the Dominican) and of that of St. Francis, residing at Tauris, Tongan, and Marogo,[2] and points out three stations adapted for the establishment of missions, viz., Supera, Paroco, and Columbum. On the receipt of these letters, Nico-

[1] "Which I suspect to be *Conengue* or *Khounouk*, a port of Persia, on the Persian Gulf," (*French Editor*). Speaking without having seen the letter, I should rather suspect it to be the island and roadstead of *Karrack*, called by the Arabs *Khârej*, but also locally, as appears by the Government charts, *Khârg*. (My friend Mr. Badger thinks it may be *El-Kât*, an ancient port still much frequented, fifty miles south-west of the mouth of the Euphrates.) I find from M. D'Avezac in *Rec. de Voyages*, (iv. 421), that this letter is published in *Quétif & Echard*, Scriptoris Ordinis Dom., i. p. 549, and that the second letter is given by *Wadding*, *Annales Minorum*, vi. 359.

[2] *Tauris*, Tabriz; *Tongan*, which the French editor calls "Djagorgan" (?), is probably Daumghan in Persia, south of Astrabad, mentioned by Marco Polo (ii. 17), with an allusion to the Chris-

laus Romanus, who was Vice-Custos of the Dominicans in Persia, is stated to have started for India.[1]

In his second letter, dated in January, 1324, Jordanus relates how he had started from Tabriz to go to Cathay, but embarked first for Columbum with four Franciscan missionaries, and how they were driven by a storm to Tana,[2] in India, where they were received by the Nestorians. There he left his companions, and started for Baroch, where he hoped to preach with success, as he was better acquainted with the Persian tongue than the others were. Being detained however at Supera, he there heard that his four brethren at Tana had been arrested, and returned to aid them, but found them already put to death. He was enabled to remove the bodies of these martyrs by the help of a young Genoese whom he found at Tana, and, having transported

tians there; and *Marogo* is Maragha in the plain east of Lake Urumia, formerly the capital of the Tartar Hulaku.

[1] Which shows that the places indicated by Jordanus were in India. Paroco is of course Baroch, and Columbum, Coulam or Quilon. Respecting the identity of this last we shall, however, have to speak more fully. Supera, the French editor states, after D'Anville, to be "the port now called Sefer, the *Sefara el Hind* of the Arabs." It is doubtless the Supara of Ptolomy, which he places on the north of the first great river south of the Namadus or Nerbudda. Masudi also says that Sefara was four days' journey from Cambay. These indications fix Supera on the Tapti, over against Surat, and probably as the ancient representative of that port. (See Reinaud's *Mém. sur la Géog. de l'Inde*, and Vincent's *Periplus of the Erythræan Sea*, p. 385.)

[2] A town on the island of Salsette, about twelve miles from Bombay, and formerly a port of considerable importance.

them to Supera, he buried them in a church there as honourably as he could.[1]

The only remaining date in the biography of Jordanus is derived from a bull of Pope John XXII., the date of which is equivalent to 5th April 1330, addressed to the Christians of Columbum, and intended to be delivered to them by Jordanus, who was nominated bishop of that place. The bull commences as follows:—[2]

"Nobili viro domino Nascarinorum et universis sub eo Christianis Nascarinis de Columbo, Venerabilem fratrem nostrum Jordanum Catalani, episcopum Columbensem, Prædicatorum Ordinis professorem, quem nuper ad episcopalis dignitatis apicem auctoritate apostolicâ duximus promovendum ——" etc.

The Pope goes on to recommend the missionaries to their goodwill, and ends by inviting the Nascarini (*Nazráni*, Christians, in India) to abjure their schism, and enter the unity of the Catholic Church.

The Pope had shortly before nominated John de Core to be Archbishop of Sultania in Persia. This metropolitan had, at least, three bishops under him, viz., of Tabriz, of Semiscat, and of Columbum.[3]

[1] According to the Acta Sanctorum of the Bollandists, this martyrdom took place, 1st April 1322. There is a letter from Francis of Pisa (I presume in the MS. above quoted), a comrade and friend of Jordanus, which gives similar details. They are also found in the *Bibliotheca Hispanica Vetus* of *Nicol. Antonio*, p. 268. (*French Editor's Comment.*) See also below, pp. ix—xii.

[2] Quoted by the French editor from *Odericus Raynaldus*, *Annal. Eccles.*, No. 55.

[3] The French editor supposes *Semiscat* to be, perhaps, a mis-

The two latter were entrusted by the Pope with the *Pallium* for the archbishop. Sultania, between Tabriz and Tehran, was the seat of the Persian kings previous to the Tartar conquest in the thirteenth century, and was still a great centre of commerce between the Indies and Europe. The number of Christians was so great, that they had in this city, it is said, four hundred churches. (?)[1]

We may suppose that Jordanus, after fulfilling his commission at Sultania, proceeded to his see in Malabar by the Persian Gulf, the route which he had followed on his first visit to India; but whether he ever reached it, or ever returned from it, seems to be undetermined.[2] M. Coquebert-Montbret assumes that he did both; but as far as I can gather, this is based on the other assumption, that his *Mirabilia* was written *after* returning a second time. My impression is that it was written *before* he went out as bishop, for it contains no allusion to his having held

reading for Samirkat = *Samarkand.* Mr. Badger suggests judiciously *Someisât,* the ancient Samosata. There was another see under Sultania, *viz.*, Verna, supposed by D'Avezac to be Orna or Ornas, which he identifies with Tana, the seat of a Venetian factory at the mouth of the Don, on the site of ancient Tanais. (*Rec. de Voy.*, iv. 510.)

[1] The editor does not give his authority for this. Sultania was destroyed by Tamerlane, and never recovered its former importance. It was still a city of some size in the time of Chardin, but is now apparently quite deserted. It is not mentioned by M. Polo.

[2] I conclude, from a passage near the end of the work (ch. xiv.), that the actual residence of Jordanus at Columbum, previous to his writing, lasted only a year, or thereabouts.

that dignity. Nor does it appear to be known whether he had any successor in his episcopate.

Another work appears to have been traced with some plausibility to our author. It is a chronicle composed in the fourteenth century, and quoted by Muratori from a MS. which in 1740 existed in the Vatican library, with the No. 1960. It is adorned with fine miniatures, and is entitled

"Satyrica gestarum rerum, regum et regnorum, atque summorum pontificum, historia, à creatione mundi usque ad Henricum VII. Romanum augustum."

The chronicle ends with the year 1320, and purports to be written by one *Jordanus*. The passage which is considered to identify him with our author is one relating to the martyrdom of four Minor Friars at Tana, and is so interesting in itself as to be worth quoting at length. It is very perplexing, that though several of the circumstances appear to identify his narrative with that which forms the subject of our author's letter quoted in a previous page, the dates are irreconcilable. This difficulty the French editor does not notice, nor can I solve it.[1]

[1] I have now no doubt that the date in the next line is wrong. For, according to M. D'Avezac (in the same volume of the *Rec. de Voyages*, which contains Jordanus, p. 417), the celebrated traveller Odoricus of Friuli, who was at Tana in 1322, sent home a letter describing this martyrdom as having occurred in the preceding year. It is in the Bib. Royale (now Impériale) at Paris. The narrative, in still greater detail than here, is indeed to be found in the Itinerary of Odoricus, as published in Hakluyt, at least in the Latin; the English translation does not give the details. From this error in date, as well as the better style of Latin, I should doubt if this chronicle was written by our Jordanus.

"MDCCCXIX. Pope John read in the consistory, with great approval, a letter which he had received, to the effect following: To wit, that certain brethren of the orders of Minors and Preachers, who had been sent on a mission to Ormus to preach the faith to the infidels, when they found that they could do no good there, thought it well to go over to Columbum in India. And when they arrived at the island called Dyo,[1] the brethren of the order of Minors separated from the rest of the party, both Preachers and secular Christians, and set out by land to a place called Thana, that they might there take ship for Columbum. Now there was at that place a certain Saracen of Alexandria, Ysufus[2] by name, and he summoned them to the presence of Melich, the governor of the land, to make inquest how and why they were come. Being thus summoned, he demands: what manner of men are ye called? They made answer, that they were Franks, devoted to holy poverty, and anxious to visit St. Thomas. Then, being questioned concerning their faith, they replied that they were true Christians, and uttered many things with holy fervour regarding the faith of Christ. But when Melich let them go, the aforesaid Yusuf a second and a third time persuaded him to arrest and detain them. At length Melich and the Cadi and the people of the place were assembled, Pagans and idolaters as well as Saracens, and questioned the brethen: How can Christ, whom ye call the Virgin's son, be the son of God, seeing that God hath not a mate? Then set they forth many instances of divine generation, as from the sun's rays, from trees, from germs in the soil; so that the infidels could not resist the Spirit who spake in them. But the

[1] Diu, on the coast of Guzerat, where the old Portuguese warriors afterwards made such a gallant defence against the "Moors" in 1547.

[2] Yusuf.

Saracens kindled a great fire, and said: Ye say that your law is better than the law of Mahomet; an it be so, go ye into the fire, and by miracle prove your words. The brethren replied that, for the honour of Christ, that they would freely do; and brother Thomas coming forward would first go in, but the Saracens suffered him not, for that he seemed older than the others; then came forward the youngest of the brethren, James of Padua, a young wrestler for Christ, and incontinently went into the fire, and abode in it until it was well nigh spent, rejoicing and uttering praise, and without any burning of his hair even, or of the cloth of his gown. Now they who stood by shouted with a great cry, Verily these be good and holy men!

"But the Cadi, willing to deny so glorious a miracle, said: It is not as ye think, but his raiment came from the land of Aben . . .[1] a great friend of God, who when cast into the flames in Chaldea, took no hurt; therefore, hath this man abode scatheless in the fire.

"Then stripped they the innocent youth, and all naked as he was born was he cast by four men into the fire. But he bore the flames without hurt, and went forth from the fire unscathed and rejoicing. Then Melich set them free to go whither they would. But the Cadi, and the aforesaid Yusuf, full of malice, knowing that they had been entertained in the house of a certain Christian, said to Melich: What dost thou? why slayest thou not these Christ-worshippers? He replied: That I find no cause of death in them. But they say: If ye let them go, all will believe in Christ, and the law of Mahomet will be utterly destroyed. Melich again says: What will ye that I should do, seeing that I find

[1] *Sic.* I suppose it should be Abraham, according to the well-known Mussulman tradition; perhaps called, as Mr. Badger kindly suggests, *Aben* (or Ibn) *Azer*, the son of Azer, the Mussulman name for Terah.

no cause of death? But they said: His blood be upon us. For it is said that if one cannot go pilgrim to Mecca, let him slay a Christian and he shall obtain a full remission of sins, as if he had visited Mecca. Wherefore, the night following, the three men aforesaid, Melich, the Cadi, and Yusuf, sent officers who despatched the three brethren, Thomas, James, and Demetrius, to the joys of heaven, bearing the palm of martyrdom. And after awhile, having made brother Peter, who was in another place, present himself before them, when he firmly held to the faith of Christ, for two days they vexed him with sore afflictions, and on the third day, cutting off his head, accomplished his martyrdom. But their comrades, the Preachers and the rest, when they heard this, wrote to the West, lamenting wofully that they had been parted from the company of the holy martyrs, and saying that they were devoutly engaged in recovering the relics of the martyrs."

I had desired to add to this preface some notices of the Christians of Malabar, embracing the latest information; but my work is cut short by circumstances, and I must content myself with saying something, hurriedly put together, as to the identity of *Columbum*, the seat of the bishop's see.

It is clear that Columbum is not Colombo in Ceylon, though the French editor is wrong in supposing that the latter city did not exist in the time of Jordanus, for it is mentioned by the modern name in Ibn Batuta's travels, only a few years later. Jordanus evidently does not speak of Ceylon as one who had been there, and whilst treating of greater India, he says distinctly, "*In istâ Indiâ, me existente in Columbo, fuerunt inventi,*" etc.

The identity of Columbum with Kulam or Quilon, on the coast of Malabar (now in Travancore), might therefore have been assumed, but for the doubts which have been raised by some of the editors of Marco Polo as to the position of the *Kulam* or *Coilon* of Marco and other medieval travellers.

Mr. Hugh Murray, adopting the view of Count Baldello Boni in his edition of Marco Polo, considers that the place so-called by those travellers was on the east coast of the Peninsula. I have not time to seek for Baldello's edition, and do not know his arguments; but I conceive that there is enough evidence to show that he is wrong.

The argument on which Murray rests is chiefly the position in which Polo introduces his description of Coilon, after Maabar, and before Comari; Maabar being with him an extensive region of Coromandel, and Comari doubtless the country about Cape Comorin. But, omitting detailed discussion of the value of this argument, which would involve a consideration of all the other difficulties in reducing to geographical order Polo's notices of the kingdoms on the coast of India, his description of Coilon as a great port for pepper and brazil-wood, is sufficient to identify it as on the coast of Malabar. The existence of places called Coulan on the east coast in the maps of D'Anville, Rennel, and Milburn, is of little moment, for an inspection of the "Atlas of India" will show scores of places so-called on both sides of Cape Comorin, the word signifying, in the Tamul tongue, 'an irrigation tank, formed by damming up natural hollows.' Indeed, though I have found no trace of any well-known port on the east coast so-called, there were at least four ports of the name on the west coast frequented by foreign vessels, viz., Cote Colam, north of Cananore; Colam, called Pandarani, north of Calicut; Cai-Colam, or Kaincolam,[1] between Cochin and the chief place of the name; Coulam, or Quilon, the Columbum of our author.

We know that Kulam, on the coast of Malabar, was founded in the ninth century, and that its foundation formed an era from which dates were reckoned in Malabar.[2] In that same century we find[3] that the sailing directions for ships making the China voyage from the Persian Gulf, were to go straight from

[1] In Keith Johnstone's new and beautiful atlas Quilon is identified with Kayan or Kain-Kulam. This, I have no doubt, is quite a mistake. The places, though near, are quite distinct, and in the beginning of the sixteenth century were under distinct sovereigns. I may here notice what I venture, with respect, to think is an error in Mr. Major's edition of Conti (*India in the Fifteenth Century*). Conti, on his first arrival in Malabar, lands at "Pudefitania," and, after describing his visit to Bengal, and his ascent of the Ganges, returns to Pudefitania. Mr. Major interprets this in the last place *Burdwan*. But, apart from other arguments, it is evidently in both passages the same place, *i.e.*, *Pudi-patanam*, one of the old forgotten ports on the coast of Mālabar, but mentioned by Barbosa and the Geographer in Ramusio. Other names mentioned by Conti are in need of examination. *Maarazia*, the great city on the Ganges which he visits, is certainly not *Muttra*, as the editor has it, but Benares. The Braminical name, *Baranási*, is near enough to Conti's.

[2] Wilson's preface to Mackenzie's Collections, p. xcviii.

[3] See the relations of Mahomedan voyagers published by Renaudot, and again by Reinaud.

Maskát to *Kulam Malé*, a place evidently, both from name and fact, on the coast of Malabar. Here there was a custom-house, where ships from China paid their dues.

The narrative of Rabbi Benjamin of Tudela is very hazy. He calls *Chulan* only seven days from El-Cathif (which is a port on the west coast of the Persian Gulf), "and on the confines of the country of the Sun-worshippers." However, his description of the pepper-gardens adjoining the city, the black Jews, etc., identify it with one of the Kulams on the Malabar coast, and doubtless with Quilon, which was the chief of them.

Then comes Polo's notice of Coilon already alluded to, followed by our author's mention of it, and residence there.

It is probable that the Polumbrum or Polembum of his contemporaries Odoricus and Mandevill, are corrupt readings of the name of Kulam or Columbum. The former describes this place as at the head of the pepper forest towards the south, and as abounding in all sorts of merchandize; Mandevill adding, "thither go merchants often from Venice to buy pepper and ginger."

Ibn Batuta, only half a century after Polo, is quite clear in his description of *Kaulam*, as the seat of an infidel king, the last city on the Malabar coast, and frequented by many Mahomedan merchants. He also says that Kaulam, Calicut, and Hílí were the only ports entered by the ships of China.

So also Conti, early in the fifteenth century, on his

return from the Eastern Archipelago, departing from Champa (Cambodia), doubtless in one of those same ships of China, after a month's voyage arrives at *Coloen*, a noble city, three days from Cochin, and "situated in the province called Melibaria."

Coming down to later times, Barbosa, in the first years of the sixteenth century, speaks of Coulon still as the great pepper port, the seat of one of the three (chief) kings of Malabar, and where lived many Moors, Gentiles, and Christians, who were great merchants, and had many ships trading to Coromandel, Ceylon, Bengal, Pegu, Malacca, Sumatra, etc.

Here, however, at last, we find something to justify Marco Polo in regard to the position in which he introduces the kingdom of Coilon. For, after speaking of Coulam on the Malabar coast, Barbosa goes forward to Cape Comorin, where he says the country of Malabar indeed terminates, but the "aforesaid kingdom of Coulam" still goes on and comes to an end at the city of Cail, where the King of Coulam made his continual residence. So also the "Summary of kingdoms," etc., in Ramusio, describes the kingdom of Colam as extending on both sides of Cape Comorin.

It is intelligible, therefore, that Marco, coming upon territory belonging to the *kingdom* of Coilon, before reaching Cape Comorin, should proceed to speak of the city of that name, though it lay upon the western coast. But there is in this no ground for asserting, as Mr. Murray does, that "the *place* of that name described by Marco and other early Europeans lay to the east of that great promontory." We have seen that a regular catena of authorities, from the ninth to the sixteenth century, concurs in representing Coulam, Kulam, Coloen, Coilon (*Quilon*), on the coast of Malabar, as the great entrepôt of trade with east and west, and there can be no reasonable doubt that this is the Columbum which was the seat of our author's mission.

The occasional quotations given in the notes will indicate the quality of the author's Latin. The French editor is unwilling to believe that episcopal Latinity could be so bad, and suggests that his vernacular was Latinized by some humbler scribe, and probably extracted from a larger work. In support of this, he adduces the abrupt commencement, and the "but" with which he plunges in—"Inter Siciliam *autem* et Calabriam." But he gives a fac-simile of the beginning of the MS., and the words seem to me (all inexpert I confess) almost certainly to be "Inter Siciliam *atque* Calabriam," so that this argument is null.

One must notice the frequent extraordinary coincidences of statement, and almost of expression, between this and other travellers of the same age, especially M. Polo. At first one would think that Jordanus had Polo's book. But he certainly had not Ibn Batuta's, and the coincidences with him are sometimes almost as striking. Had those ancient worthies, then, a MURRAY from whom they pilfered experiences, as modern travellers do? I think they had; but *their* Murray lay in the traditional yarns of the Arab sailors with whom they voyaged, some of which seem to have been handed down steadily from the time of Ptolemy—peradventure of Herodotus[1]—almost to our own day.

And so I commend the simple and zealous Jordanus to kindly entertainment.

[1] See end of note to ch. v. para. 16.

London, June 27th, 1863.

NOTA BENE. The English edition of Marco Polo, so often referred to in my notes, is Mr. Hugh Murray's fourth edition; Edinburgh, Oliver and Boyd, (*no date;* more shame to Oliver and Boyd).

In my absence on the continent my friend Mr. Badger has undertaken the correction of the press. The *revise* sheets have been sent to me, but in the absence of my manuscript and references I fear some errors may still inevitably escape correction.

The numbers to chapters and paragraphs have been attached by me,

H. Y.

MARVELS DESCRIBED

BY

FRIAR JORDANUS,

OF THE ORDER OF PREACHERS, NATIVE OF SEVERAC, AND BISHOP OF COLUMBUM IN INDIA THE GREATER.

I.

1. Between Sicily and Calabria there is a marvel in the sea. This is it: on one side the sea runneth with an upward current, and on the other side cometh down towards the island with a swifter stream than any river; and so in the middle is caused a wondrous eddy, sucking down ships that hap to fall in with it, whatever be their bigness. And 'tis said that in the bottom of the sea there is a horrid kind of a whirlpool, from which the water cometh forth so wondrous dark that even the fishes nowhere dare to come near it.[1]

[1] Admiral Smyth says that the currents in the Faro are so numerous and varied, that it is difficult to ascertain anything precise about them. In settled seasons a central stream runs north and south, at the rate of two to five miles an hour. On each shore there is a *refluo*, or counter-set, often forming eddies to the central current. When the main current runs to the north it is called *Rema montante*, or flood; when it runs south, *Rema scendente*, or ebb; and this has obtained, perhaps, even from the days of Eratosthenes. He considers that the *special* danger from the Faro currents

2. In Greece I neither saw nor heard of aught worth telling, unless it be that between the island of Negropont and the mainland the sea ebbeth and floweth sometimes thrice, sometimes four times, sometimes oftener, like a rapid river; and that is a marvel to be sure![1]

3. I was at Thebes, where there be so many earthquakes that nobody could believe it who had not felt them; for it will happen five, or six, or seven times in the twenty-four

is insignificant. There are dangerous *squalls* from the ravines or river-beds on the high Calabrian coast.

He admits some little more of reality in the celebrated vortex of Charybdis, which must have been formidable to the undecked vessels of the ancients; for in the present day small craft are sometimes endangered, and he has seen even a seventy-four whirled round on its surface. The "Galofaro" appears to be an agitated water of from seventy to ninety fathoms in depth, circling in quick eddies, but rather an incessant undulation than a whirlpool, and the cases are only extreme when any vortiginous ripples threaten danger to laden boats. "It is owing probably to the meeting of the harbour and lateral currents with the main one, the latter being forced over in this direction by the opposite point of Pezzo. This agrees in some measure with the relation of Thucydides, who calls it a violent reciprocation of the Tyrrhene and Sicilian seas, and he is the only writer of remote antiquity I remember to have read who has assigned this danger its true situation, and not exaggerated its effects." (*Abridged from* Smyth's *Mediterranean*, pp. 180-1). Our author seems to mix up the two phenomena in his exaggerated account. The *upward and downward current* suggest that he had heard the local terms quoted by Admiral Smyth.

[1] "The breadth of the Euripus is diminished by a rock in mid-channel, on which a fort is built, dividing it into two channels: that towards the main, though rather the broader, is only practicable for small boats, as there is not more than three feet water at any time. Between the rock and the walls of Egripos is a distance of 33 feet, and the least depth at the highest water is 7 feet. It is here that the extraordinary tides take place for which the Euripus was formerly so noted; at times the water runs as much as eight miles an hour, with a fall under the bridge of 1½ foot; but what is most singular is, that vessels lying 150 yards from the bridge are not the least affected by this rapid. It remains but a short time in a quiescent state, changing its direction in a few minutes, and almost immediately resuming its velocity, which is generally from four to five miles an hour either way, its greatest rapidity being, however, always to the southward. The results of three months' observation, in which the above phenomena were noted, afforded no sufficient data for reducing them to any regularity"—*Penny Cyclop.*, Article *Eubœa*. See also *Leake* (*Tr. in Northern Greece*, ii. p. 257), who quotes Wheler and Spon.

hours, many a time and oft, that the strongest houses and walls shall be thrown down by earthquakes.[1]

II.

HERE FOLLOWETH CONCERNING ARMENIA.

1. In Armenia the Greater I saw one great marvel. This is it: a mountain of excessive height and immense extent, on which Noah's ark is said to have rested. This mountain is never without snow, and seldom or never without clouds, which rarely rise higher than three parts up. The mountain is inaccessible, and there never has been anybody who could get farther than the edge of the snow.[2] And (marvellous indeed!) even the beasts chased by the huntsmen, when they come to the snow, will liefer turn, will liefer yield them into the huntsmen's hands, than go farther up that mountain.

[1] Greece generally is subject to earthquakes, but I cannot find evidence that Thebes is particularly so.

[2] The first ascent of Ararat is well known to have been made by Professor Parrot, of Dorpat, 9th October, 1829, whose account of his journey has been translated by Mr. Cooley.

"From the summit downwards, for nearly two-thirds of a mile perpendicular, or nearly three miles in an oblique direction, it is covered with a crown of eternal snow and ice" (*Parrot's Journey*, p. 133). As to the clouds, the same author remarks with regard to a drawing of Ararat: "The belt of clouds about the mountain is characteristic" (p. 137). And Smith and Dwight (*Researches in Armenia*, p. 266) say that they were prevented by clouds from seeing it for three weeks. It is believed in the country that the Ark still exists on the mountain, access to which has been forbidden by Divine decree since Noah's time. A holy monk called Jacob resolved to convince himself by inspection. But in his ascent of the mountain he three times was overtaken by sleep, and each time found that he had unconsciously lost the ground that he had gained when awake. At last an angel came to him when again asleep, and told him that his zeal was fruitless, but was to be rewarded by a fragment of the wood of the Ark, a sacred relic still preserved in the Cathedral of Echmiazin. (*Parrot*, and *Smith and Dwight*); see also the narrative of *Guillaume de Rubruk* (Rubruquis), in *Rec. de Voyages*, iv. p. 387.

This mountain hath a compass of more than three days journey for a man on horseback going without halt. There be serpents of a great size, which swallow hares alive and whole, as I heard from a certain trustworthy gentleman who saw the fact, and shot an arrow at a serpent with a hare in his mouth, but scathed it not.[1] In a certain part of the mountain is a dwelling which Noah is said to have built on leaving the ark; and there, too, is said to be that original vine which Noah planted, and whereby he got drunk; and it giveth such huge branches of grapes as you would scarce believe. This I heard from a certain Catholic archbishop of ours, a great man and a powerful, and trustworthy to boot, the lord of that land; and, indeed, I believe I have been at the place myself, but it was in the winter season.[2]

2. This country of Armenia the Greater is very extensive, and there three of the apostles suffered martyrdom: Bartholomew, Simon, and Judas. I saw a prison in which the two latter apostles were kept; and likewise springs of water which they produced from the living rock, smiting it with

[1] Stories of serpents seem to be rife in Armenia. On the Araxes, south of Nakhcheván (see note below), is a mountain called the Serpent Mountain, where serpents are said to collect in such numbers at certain times, that no man or beast dare approach. (See *Haxthausen's Transcaucasia*, pp. 144, 181, 353, etc.)

[2] The name of the province and town of *Nakhcheván*, east of Ararat, signifies "first place of descent, or of lodging." The antiquity of the tradition is proved by the fact, that Josephus affirms that the Armenians call the place where the Ark rested "*the place of descent*;" whilst Ptolemy supplies the name of *Naxuana*. (*Smith and Dwight*, p. 255.)

The place alluded to by Jordanus appears to be Arguri, the only village upon Ararat. Here Noah is said to have built his altar on the exact spot now occupied by the church, and it is of the vineyards of Arguri that the Scripture is believed to speak when it is said that "Noah began to be an husbandman, and planted a vineyard." The church is of unascertained but remote date; and the name of the place signifies *(Argh-urri)* "He planted the vine." (*Parrot*, p. 122.) At Nakhcheván "the grapes were almost unequalled in excellence, and seemed to deserve the honour of growing on the spot." (*Smith and Dwight*, p. 256.) Arguri was buried by an earthquake, accompanied by volcanic indications, July 2nd, 1840. *(Smith's Dict. of the Bible, Art. Ararat.)*

a rod VIII times, or X times, or XVII times (anyhow there be just as many springs as there were blows struck); and hard by there was a church built, beauteous and of wonderful bigness.[1]

3. In this same Armenia the Greater a certain glorious virgin suffered martyrdom, the daughter of a king, and Scala by name.[2] And there, too, was cast into a well, with a lion and a dragon, St. Gregory, who converted Armenia to the Catholic faith, as well as its king Tertal,[3] in the time of St. Sylvester and the Emperor Constantine.[4] In this Armenia, too, was slain the blessed martyr Jacobus.

4. This province is inhabited chiefly by schismatic Armenians, but the Preaching and Minor friars have converted a good four thousand of them, and more. For one archbishop, a great man, called the Lord Zachary, was converted with his whole people; and we trust in the Lord that in a short

[1] The Armenian belief is, that Thaddeus, one of the Seventy, was, after the Ascension, sent by St. Thomas, according to commands given him by the Lord, to Abgarus of Edessa, who had written the celebrated letter. Thaddeus, and Bartholomew who followed him, were successively put to death by Sanatruk, the heathen nephew of Abgarus. Jude also came to preach in Armenia, and was put to death in Ormi (Urumia). The mission of Simon I do not find mentioned, but Chardin states that his body was said to be preserved in one of the churches. (See *Avdall's* Tr. of *Chamich's Hist. of Armenia*. Calcutta, 1827, pp. 107-111, and *Smith and Dwight.*)

[2] The virgin must be *Rhipsime*, said to have been of the house of Claudius Cæsar, who, with Kayane and thirty-seven other holy virgins, were put to death in the time of Dioclesian. There are churches dedicated to R. and K. at Echmiazin. *(Smith and Dwight.)*

[3] Tertal is Tiridates, in Armenian Dertad=Theodosius. *(Smith and Dwight.)*

[4] St. Gregory, called The Illuminator, born A.D. 257, consecrated Archbishop of Armenia 302. He is said to have revived (probably *introduced*) Christianity in Armenia, and, after suffering persecution at the hands of King Tiridates, converted him and his whole people. The place alluded to by Jordanus is at the convent of Khor-virab ("Deep pit"), on the Araxes, under Ararat. Here Gregory is believed to have been confined in a cave with serpents, and in the endurance of manifold torments, for fourteen years. (*Smith and Dwight*, p. 273. See also *Chardin*, p. 251. *Curzon's Armenia* has a concise account of the Armenian church.)

time the whole residue shall be converted also, if only the good friars go on so.[1]

5. There are many good and great Armenian princes, Christians; but the Persian emperor hath the paramount sovereignty.[2]

6. In this Armenia there is a Dead Sea, very bitter to the taste, where they say there be no fish at all, and which cannot be sailed upon by reason of the stench; and it has an island where are buried many ancient emperors and kings of the Persians, with an infinity of treasure; but nobody is allowed to go there, or, if allowed, they dare not search for the treasure.[3]

7. This Armenia extendeth in length from Sebast to the Plain of Mogan and the Caspian Mountains; and in breadth from the Barcarian Mountains to Tabriz,[4] which is a good twenty-three days' journey, the length being more than forty days.[5]

[1] "The ancient and extensive Dominican mission, which once had its seat in this province, (Nakhchevan) is now no more. It was commenced about 1320 by an Italian papal monk of the Dominican order. Such success attended it that soon nearly thirty Armenian villages embraced the faith of Rome, and acknowledged subjection to a papal bishop, who after being consecrated at Rome resided in the village of Aburan, with the title of Archbishop of Nakhcheván." (*Smith and Dwight*, p. 257.)

[2] At this time a Tartar successor of Hulaku.

[3] This Dead Sea is doubtless the Lake of Urumia, the waters of which are salter than sea water. It appears to be about ninety miles in length from north to south. There are no fish in it. It contains several islands, or peninsulas which are occasionally islands, two of which have been used as fortresses. In one of these Hulaku the Tartar conqueror of Baghdad was said to have stored his treasures. Another is said to be "as old as the days of Zoroaster," who is believed to have been born in the vicinity. I do not find tombs mentioned. (*Penny Cyc.* in v. *Azerbijan*, also *Monteith* in *Jour. Geog. Soc.* iii. 55, and *Smith and Dwight*, 348.)

[4] "*Thaurisium.*"

[5] Sebast is doubtless Sivas, called by Marco Polo Sebastos, anciently Sebasteia (*Smith's Dict. of Gr. and Rom. Geo.*) south of Tokat, and giving name to a pachalik. The Barcarian mountains appear as *Barchal Dagh* running parallel to the Black Sea between Trebisond and Kars. (*Stieler's Hand-Atlas*, 43a.) Mogan is *Orogan* in the original, but, as we shall see below, this is an error of transcription. The *Plain* of Mogan is the great

8. There is a certain lake, at the foot of the aforesaid great mountain, where ten thousand martyrs were martyred, and in their martyrdom happened all the same tokens as in the Passion of Christ, for that they all were crucified for Christ.[1] And that part of the mountain is called Ararat; and there was a city there called Semur, exceeding great, which was destroyed by the Tartars.[2] I have been over all that country,—almost.

9. But I saw not anything else, in this Armenia the greater, worth telling as a marvel.

III.

HERE FOLLOWETH CONCERNING THE REALM OF PERSIA.

1. In Persia, however, I saw a very marvellous thing: to wit, that in Tabriz, which is a very great city, containing as many as two hundred thousand houses,[3] dew never falls

plain extending from the eastern foot of Caucasus along the Caspian, and stretching to the south of the Cyrus and Araxes. Here Pompey's career eastward is said to have been arrested by the venomous serpents with which the long grass of the plain is infested. The dread of these serpents still exists. "Their hissing is heard from afar, and they seem to rise from the grass like fish from the sea", Kinneir was told. Here the camp of Heraclius was pitched, as was that of the Tartar hosts for many months during their invasion of Armenia in the thirteenth century, and that of Nadir Shah when he placed the crown upon his head. (*Macd. Kinneir's Mem. of Persia*, 153; *Avdall's Hist. of Armenia.*)

[1] The Lake appears to be Gokchai or Sevan, north-east of Erivan. There is a small island with a monastery upon it. There are many traditions attached to the monasteries in this vicinity, but I cannot find this one.

[2] Perhaps Erivan, but I cannot trace the name.

[3] Sir John Chardin (356) says he may "truly reck'n" the population of Tauris to be 550,000 persons, and that several in the city would have it to be double that number! yet he had said just before that it contained 15,000 houses and 15,000 shops, so that 150,000 souls would be a liberal estimate. It appears now to contain from 30,000 to 50,000. Kinneir calls it one of the most wretched cities in Persia. Such estimates of city popu-

from heaven; nor doth it rain in summer as in most parts it doth, but they water artificially everything that is grown for man's food.[1] There also, or thereabouts, on a kind of willows, are found certain little worms, which emit a liquid which congeals upon the leaves of the tree, and also drops upon the ground, white like wax; and that excretion is sweeter than honey and the honeycomb.[2]

2. There we have a fine-enough church, and about a thousand of the schismatics converted to our faith, and about as

lation are common enough still. Many books and many gentlemen in India will still tell us that Benares contains half a million, and that Lucknow before 1857 contained 700,000; the fact being, as regards Benares, that by *census* and including its suburbs it contains 171,668; whilst the estimate for Lucknow was probably five or six times the truth. I suspect the usual estimate of 000,000 in the city of Madras to be of equal value.

[1] At Tabriz "dew is entirely unknown, and not more than two or three showers fall between March and December. The plain around is very fertile where irrigated." (*Penny Cyc.*)

[2] The only manna I have known in India was exuded by a tamarisk; but it appears to be produced on various shrubs in Persia and the adjoining countries, camelthorns, tamarisks, and others. And one kind called *Bed-kisht* is produced on a species of willow. (*Bed* signifies a *willow*.) Some kinds of manna are used as sugar. (See *Pen. Cyc.* in v. *Manna.*) This authority does not seem to recognize the agency of any insect in its production. But Macdonald Kinneir (in his *Memoir of the Persian Empire*, p. 329) has the following note. "Manna is exported from Moosh, on the Euphrates [west of Lake Van] in considerable quantities. It is termed *guz* by the Persians, and found in great quantities in Louristan, and in the district of Khonsar in Irak. It is taken from a small shrub, in appearance not unlike a funnel, about four feet in height and three in diameter at the top. The *guz* is said to be produced by small insects, which are seen to move in vast numbers under the small and narrow leaves of the shrub.—These were always in motion, and continued to crawl between the bark and the leaves. The *guz* is collected during the months of August and September in the following manner. A vessel of an oval form being placed under the bush as a receptacle, the leaves are beat every third day with a crooked stick covered with leather. The manna when first gathered has the tenacity and appearance of gum, but, when exposed to the heat of 90° of Fahrenheit's thermometer, it dissolves into a liquid resembling honey. When mixed with sweetmeat its tenacity resists the application of the knife, but when suddenly struck it shivers into pieces."

many also in Ur of the Chaldees, where Abraham was born, which is a very opulent city, distant about two days from Tabriz.[1]

3. Likewise also at Sultania we have five hundred, or five hundred and fifty. This is eight days' distant from Tabriz, and we have a very fine church there.

4. In this country of Persia are certain animals called *onagri,* which are like little asses, but swifter in speed than our horses.[2]

5. This Persia is inhabited by Saracens and Saracenized Tartars, and by schismatic Christians of divers sects, such as Nestorians, Jacobites, Greeks, Georgians, Armenians, and by a few Jews. Persia hath abundance of silk, and also of ultramarine,[3] but they wot not how to prepare it. They have likewise exceeding much gold in the rivers, but they wot not how to extract it, nor be they worthy to do so.

6. Persia extendeth about V[4] days' journey in length, and as much in breadth. The people of this realm live all too uncleanly, for they sit upon the ground, and eke eat upon the same, putting mess and meats[5] in a trencher for

[1] There is a town called in the maps *Ahar,* about fifty miles north-east of Tabriz, but I cannot find that this was ever considered to be Ur of the Chaldees. Urfa, which is generally supposed to be Ur, is in quite another region, more than four hundred miles from Tabriz.

[2] Wild asses are found in the dry regions from the frontiers of Syria to the Runn of Cutch, and north to 48° lat. Ferrier mentions herds of hundreds between Mushid and Herat, and on the banks of the Khashrood, south of Herat. "They are fleet as deer," he says. Their flesh is more delicate than Persian beef, and the Afghans consider it a great delicacy, as did the old Roman epicures. This species, as I learn from a note with which Mr. Moore, of the India Museum, has kindly favoured me, is *Asinus Onager,* the *Kulan* or *Ghor-khar* of the Persians. That of Syria and Northern Arabia is the *Asinus Hemippus,* the Hemionus of the ancients; whilst the *Kyang* or *Jiggetai* (*Equus Hemionus* of Pallas, *E. Polyodon* of Hodgson) inhabits Tibet and thence northward to southern Siberia; and the true wild ass (*E. asinus*) is indigenous to north-eastern Africa, and perhaps to south Arabia and the island of Socotra.

[3] "*Lapis azurii,*" hod. *lapis lazuli.* Quantities of this are found in Badakshan. (*Burnes, Bokhara,* ii. 205. 8vo ed.)

[4] *Sic.* Probably L, or LV is intended.

[5] "*Ferculum et carnem.*"

three, four, or five persons together. They eat not on a table-cloth,[1] but on a round sheet of leather, or on a low table of wood or brass, with three legs. And so six, seven, or eight persons eat out of one dish, and that with their hands and fingers; big and little, male and female, all eat after this fashion. And after they have eaten, or even whilst in the middle of their eating, they lick their fingers with tongue and lips, and wipe them on their sleeves,[2] and afterwards, if any grease still remains upon their hands, they wipe them on their shoes. And thus do the folk over all those countries, including Western and Eastern Tartary, except the Hindus, who eat decently enough, though they too eat with their hands.[3]

7. In Persia are some springs, from which flows a kind of pitch, which is called *kic*[4] *(pix, dico, seu Pegua)*, with which they smear the skins in which wine is carried and stored.

8. Between this country of Persia and India the Less is a certain region where manna falls in a very great quantity, white as snow, sweeter than all other sweet things, delicious, and of an admirable and incredible efficacy. There are also sandhills in great numbers, and very destructive to men; for when the wind blows, the sand flows down just like water from a tank.[5] These countries aforesaid, to wit,

[1] "*Tobalia.*"

[2] The Afghans exceed the practices here graphically described; for they, I believe, often expectorate in the hairy sleeve of the *postin*, which in winter they wear after the fashion of Brian O'Linn, "with the leather side out and the woolly side in." Scott Waring (*Tour to Shiraz*, p. 103) notices the dirty table habits of the Persians.

[3] The friar's remarks seem to shew that forks were common in Europe earlier than is generally represented to be the case.

[4] No doubt it should be *kir*, which is bituminous pitch in Persian. What the parenthesis means I cannot make out. *Pegua* can scarcely be a reference to the petroleum of Pegu at this early date?

[5] Burnes describes the vast fields of soft sand, formed into ridges, between Bokhara and the Oxus. Their uniformity is remarkable, all having the shape of a horse-shoe, convex towards the north, from which

Persia, Armenia Major, Chaldeia, as well as Cappadocia and Asia Minor and Greece, abound in good fruits, meats, and other things, like our own country; but their lands are not so populous,—no, not a tithe,—except Greece.

IV.

CONCERNING INDIA THE LESS.[1]

1. In the entrance to India the Less are [date] palms, giving a very great quantity of the sweetest fruit; but further on in India they are not found.[2]

the prevailing wind blows. On this side they slope, inside they are precipitous. The height is from fifteen to twenty feet. "The particles of sand, moving from one mound to another, wheeling in the eddy or interior of the semicircle, and having now and then, particularly under the rays of the sun, much the look of water, an appearance, I imagine, which has given rise to the opinion of moving sands in the desert." (*Bokhara*, ii. pp. 1, 2.)

Our author may possibly have heard of the *Reg-rawán*, or "flowing sand," of the Koh Daman, near Istalif. (See *Wood's Oxus*, p. 181.)

[1] It may be gathered from what follows, that Lesser India embraces Sindh, and probably Mekran, and India along the coast as far as some point immediately north of Malabar. Greater India extends from Malabar very indefinitely to the eastward, for he makes it include Champa (Cambodia). India Tertia is the east of Africa.

According to the old Portuguese geographer, whose "Summary of Kingdoms," etc., is given by Ramusio, *First India* (see text, next page), ends at Mangalore, *Second India* at the Ganges.

Marco Polo reverses the titles given by our author. He makes Greater India extend from Maabar (south part of the Coromandel coast) to Kesmacoran (Kidj-mekrán or Mekran), whilst Lesser India stretches from the Coromandel to Champa. Abyssinia, Marco calls *Middle India*. (See *Murray's Polo*, pt. ii. ch. xxxvi.) Benjamin of Tudela speaks of "Middle India which is called Aden." Conti says all India is divided into three parts, the first extending from Persia (Ormus ?) to the Indus, the second from the Indus to the Ganges, the third all beyond.

It is worth noting that Pliny says it was disputed whether Gedrosia (Mekran), etc., belonged to India or to Ariana. (vi. p. 23.)

[2] I believe this is substantially correct. Sindh is the only province in India that produces edible dates. A date-palm is found all over India, but the fruit is worthless.

2. In this lesser India are many things worthy to be noted with wonder; for there are no springs, no rivers, no ponds; nor does it ever rain, except during three months, viz., between the middle of May and the middle of August; and (wonderful!) notwithstanding this, the soil is most kindly and fertile, and during the nine months of the year in which it does not rain, so much dew is found every day upon the ground that it is not dried up by the sun's rays till the middle of the third hour of the day.[1]

3. Here be many and boundless marvels; and in this First India beginneth, as it were, another world; for the men and women be all black, and they have for covering nothing but a strip of cotton tied round the loins, and the end of it flung over the naked back. Wheaten bread is there not eaten by the natives, although wheat they have in plenty; but rice is eaten with its seasoning,[2] only boiled in water. And they have milk and butter and oil, which they often eat uncooked. In this India there be no horses, nor mules, nor camels, nor elephants; but only kine, with which they do all their doings that they have to do, whether it be riding, or carrying, or field labour. The asses are few in number and very small, and not much worth.[3]

4. The days and nights do not vary there more than by two hours at the most.

[1] Till half-past nine o'clock. "*Quod usque ad mediam tertiam per solis radios ullâtenus possit desiccari.*" "The dews" in Lower Sindh, says Burnes, "are very heavy and dangerous." (iii. p. 254.) The fertility of the country is, however, confined to the tracts inundated or irrigated from the Indus and its branches. As to the absence of rain, Dr. Lord says, that the rainfall registered by Lt. Wood during one year at Hyderabad was only 2·55 inches, whilst at Larkhana, further north, a shower of rain which fell after the arrival of Burnes's party was universally ascribed to the good fortune of the Firingis, as for three years, the natives said, rain had scarcely been known." (*Reports and Papers on Sindh*, etc.—Calcutta, 1839, p. 61.)

[2] "*Risis autem comeditur atque sagina in aquâ tantummodo cocta.*"

[3] He is wrong about the non-existence of horses and camels in what he calls India the Less.

5. There be always fruits and flowers there, divers trees, and fruits of divers kinds; for (example) there are some trees which bear very big fruit, called *Chaqui;* and the fruit is of such size that one is enough for five persons.[1]

[1] Five persons to *eat,* that is. But an English gentleman, who is a coffee planter in the middle of Java, told me that he once cut a jack (the fruit intended by the bishop), which it took *three* men to *carry.* That they grow in Ceylon to 50 lbs. weight at least is testified by Cordiner and Sir Emerson Tennent. The former says they grow there to two feet in length, and to the same circumference, which is bigger than I ever saw them in Bengal. The manner of growing is accurately described in the next paragraph of the text.

The jack is, no doubt, the Indian fruit described by Pliny, Book xii. ch. 12, as putting forth its fruit from the bark, and as being remarkable for the sweetness of its juice, a single one containing enough to satisfy four persons. The name of the tree, he says, is *pala,* and of the fruit *Ariena.* The former is possibly the Tamul name, *Pila,* which is also one of the Malabar names. If, however, Pliny derived the whole of his information on this fruit, as he appears to derive part of it, from the historians of the Alexandrian invasion, the name may be merely the Sanskrit *phala,* a fruit, and it would be a comical illustration of the persistency of Indian habits of mind. For a stranger in India asking the question, "What is that?" would almost certainly at this day receive for reply, "*P'hal hai, khudáwand!*" "It is a *fruit,* my lord!"

The name *jack,* which we give to the tree and its fruits, is one of that large class of words which are neither English nor Hindustani, but *Anglo-Indian,* and the origin of which is often very difficult to trace. Drury gives *Pilavoo* as the Malayalim name, but I find that Rheede (*Hortus Malabaricus,* vol. iii.) gives also *Tsjaka;* and Linschoten, too, says that the jack is in Malabar called Iaca: so here we have doubtless the original.

I was long puzzled by the two species of our author, *Chaqui* and *Bloqui.* There are, indeed, two well-known species of artocarpus giving fruits which are both edible, and have a strong external resemblance, the jack and the breadfruit. But the breadfruit is *not* as big, *not* as sweet, and does *not* bear its fruit from the trunk and roots, but from twigs. Nor is it grown in Malabar, though sometimes, Ainslie says *(Materia Medica),* imported from Ceylon for sale. No *modern* authors that I can find make a clear distinction of kinds of jack. But, on referring back, we find that all the old authors, who really seem to have gone into these practical matters with more freshness and sympathy in native tastes, do so. Thus Linschoten says, "There are two sorts of them: the best are called *Girasal,* and the common or least esteemed *Chambasal,* though in fashion and trees there is no difference, save that the Girasals have a sweeter taste;" and his old commentator, "the learned Doctor Paludanus, of Enckhuysen," says, also, there are "two sorts, and the best is called *Barca,* the other *Papa,* which is not so good, and yet in handling is soft like the other." Nearly three

6. There is another tree which has fruit like that just named, and it is called *Bloqui*, quite as big and as sweet, but not of the same species. These fruits never grow upon the twigs, for these are not able to bear their weight, but only from the main branches, and even from the trunk of the tree itself, down to the very roots.

7. There is another tree which has fruit like a plum, but a very big one, which is called *Aniba*. This is a fruit so sweet and delicious as it is impossible to utter in words.[1]

8. There be many other fruit trees of divers kinds, which it would be tedious to describe in detail.

9. I will only say this much, that this India, as regards

hundred years earlier Ibn Batuta had said, that of the fruits of India "are those termed *Shaki* and *Barki*,......the fruit grows out from the bottom of the tree, and that which grows nearest to the earth is called the Barki; it is extremely sweet and well-flavoured in taste; what grows above this is called the Shaki," etc. Lastly, we have Rheede, speaking with authority, "Ceterum arboris hujus ultra triginta numerantur species ratione fructuum distinctæ, *quæ tamen omnes ad duo referentur genera;* quorum alterius fructus qui carne succulentâ, gratissimi, melliniquc saporis turgent, *varaka;* at alterius, qui carne flaccidâ, molliori et minus sapidâ referti sunt, *Tsjakapa* nuncupantur." (iii. p. 19.) Drury, indeed, says, "There are several varieties, but what is called the Honeyjack is by far the sweetest and best."

To conclude this long discourse on a short text, it seems certain that the *Bloqui* of our author is the *Barki* of Ibn Batuta, the *Barka* of Paludanus, the *Varaka* "mellini saporis" of Rheede, and the Honeyjack of Drury. "He that desireth to see more hereof let him reade *Lodouicus Romanus,* in his fifth Booke and fifteene Chapter of his Nauigatiouns, and *Christopherus a Costa* in his Cap. of *Iaca,* and *Gracia ab Horto,* in the second Booke and fourth Chapter," saith the learned Paludanus,—and so say I, by all means!

[1] *Amba* (Pers.), the Mango. Ibn Batuta writes it *'anbâ* with an *'ain,* as appears from Lee's note (p. 104), and the latter translates it "grape," which is the meaning of that word I believe in *Arabic.* Our author's just description of the flavour of the mango is applicable, however, only to the finer stocks, and seems to show that the "Bombay mango" already existed in the thirteenth century. The mango is commonly believed in Anglo-India to produce boils, which I see was also the belief in Linschoten's day. But I agree with his commentator, that, at the time when the fruit is ripe, "by reason of the great heate and season of the yeare—many doe fall into the forenamed diseases, although they eate none of this fruite."

fruit and other things, is entirely different from Christendom; except, indeed, that there be lemons there, in some places, as sweet as sugar, whilst there be other lemons sour like ours.[1] There be also pomegranates, but very poor and small. There be but few vines, and they make from them no wine, but eat the fresh grapes; albeit there are a number of other trees whose sap they collect, and it standeth in place of wine to them.

10. First of these is a certain tree called *Nargil;*[2] which tree every month in the year sends out a beautiful frond like [that of] a [date] palm-tree, which frond or branch produces very large fruit, as big as a man's head. There often grow on one such stem thirty of those fruits as big as I have said. And both flowers and fruits are produced at the same time, beginning with the first month and going up gradually to the twelfth; so that there are flowers and fruit in eleven stages of growth to be seen together. A wonder! and a thing which cannot be well understood without being witnessed.[3] From these branches and fruits is drawn a very sweet water. The kernel [at first] is very tender and pleasant to eat; afterwards it waxeth harder, and a milk is drawn from it as good as milk of almonds; and when the kernel waxeth harder still, an oil is made from it of great medicinal

[1] This would seem to imply that the orange was not known in Southern Europe in the author's time; though there are such things as sweet lemons.

[2] The Persian name for the coco-nut, and coco-palm.

[3] So Ibn Batuta—"Of this sort of trees the palm will produce fruit twelve times in the year, each month supplying a fresh crop: so that you will see upon the trees the fruit of some large, of others small, of others dry, and of others green. And this is the case always." (See p. 176.)

The account of the coco-palm, though slightly mythicized, is substantially correct. In the third year of the palm's growth the fronds begin to fall, a new frond appearing at the end of every month. Of these there are twenty-eight, more or less, on a full-grown tree. On a single tree there are about twelve branches, or spadices, of nuts. Most of the young fruit falls off, only a few coming to perfection; but as from ten to fifteen nuts *on an average* are produced on one branch, a single tree may produce eighty to one hundred nuts every year. *(Drury's Useful Plants of India.)*

virtue. And if any one careth not to have fruit, when the fruit-bearing stem is one or two months old he maketh a cut in it, and bindeth a pot to this incision; and so the sap, which would have been converted into fruit, drops in; and it is white like milk, and sweet like must, and maketh drunk like wine, so that the natives do drink it for wine; and those who wish not to drink it so, boil it down to one-third of its bulk, and then it becometh thick, like honey; and 'tis sweet, and fit for making preserves, like honey and the honeycomb.[1] One branch gives one potful in the day and one in the night, on the average throughout the year:[2] thus five or six pots may be found hung upon the same tree at once. With the leaves of this tree they cover their houses during the rainy season.[3] The fruit is that which we call *nuts of India;* and from the rind of that fruit is made the twine with which they stitch their boats together in those parts.[4]

11. There is another tree of a different species, which like that gives all the year round a white liquor pleasant to drink, which tree is called *Tari.*[5] There is also another, called *Bel-*

[1] This is the *jaggeri*, or palm-sugar, used extensively in southern India. It is made by boiling down the fresh toddy over a slow fire. The description of the extraction of the toddy, etc., is substantially correct.

[2] "*Omni tempore mundi, et hoc sicut venit.*"

[3] The leaves are employed for thatching houses, especially in Malabar." (*Drury*, p. 152.)

[4] The well known *coir*. The native practice is to steep the husk in salt water for eighteen months or two years before beating out the *coir;* but this has been proved to be injurious. The virtues of *coir* are strength, lightness, elasticity, durability, power of standing sea-water. It is now largely used in England for brushes, mats, carpets, etc. (*Drury.*)

[5] Persian *Tár*. *Tádi* is the Teloogoo name, according to Drury; in Hindustani, *tár* and *tál*. It is the palmyra (*Borassus flabelliformis*), a tree found from Malabar along the coast to Bengal, and thence down the transgangetic coast through Burma and the great islands, and also up the Ganges to Cawnpore, a little above which it ceases. The fruit is of no value. The wood is much used for rafters, etc., and it is better than that of any other Indian palm; but the tree is chiefly used for the derivation of the liquor to which, as taken from this and other palms, we give the slightly corrupted name of *toddy*, a name which in Scotland has received a new application. It is the tree from which palm-sugar is most generally

luri, giving a liquor of the same kind, but better.[1] There be also many other trees, and wonderful ones; among which is one which sendeth forth roots from high up, which gradually grow down to the ground and enter it, and then wax into trunks like the main trunk, forming as it were an arch; and by this kind of multiplication one tree will have at once as many as twenty or thirty trunks beside one another, and all connected together. 'Tis marvellous! And truly this which I have seen with mine eyes, 'tis hard to utter with my tongue. The fruit of this tree is not useful, but poisonous and deadly.[2]

made. The leaves are used for making fans (the typical fan being evidently a copy of this leaf), for writing on, and in some places for thatching, etc.

[1] *Belluri* I conceive to be the *Caryota urens*, which, according to Rheede *Hortus Malabar.*, i.), is called by the Brahmans in Malabar *tirala*. Most of our author's names seem to be Persian in form; but there is probably no Persian name for this palm. Richardson, however, has "*barhal*, name of a tree and its fruit." This tree yields more toddy than any other palm, as much as a hundred pints in twenty-four hours. Much sugar is made from it, especially in Ceylon. It also affords a sago, and a fibre for fishing lines, known in England as "Indian gut." A woolly stuff found at the springing of the fronds, is said by Drury to be used for caulking. I may add that it makes an excellent *amadou* for smokers; but the specific name does not come from this fact, as I have heard suggested, but from the burning acridity of the fruit when applied to the tongue. The *caryota*, with its enormous jagged fronds, and huge pendulous bunches of little bead-like berries, is a very beautiful object. The fruit is actually used for beads by the Mahomedans. Buchanan (*Mysore*, etc., ii, 454) says its leaves are the favourite food of the elephant, and that its sugar is superior to that of the palmyra, but inferior to that of the cocoa nut.

[2] The banyan:

"Such as at this day, to Indians known
In Malabar or Decan, spreads her arms
Branching so broad and long, that in the ground
The bended twigs take root, and daughters grow
About the mother-tree, a pillared shade
High over-arched, and echoing walks between:
There oft the Indian herdsman, shunning heat,
Shelters in cool, and tends his pasturing herds
At loopholes cut through thicket shade."

(*Paradise Lost*, b. ix.)

Which noble lines are almost an exact versification of Pliny's description (xii, 11). Drury quotes Roxburgh as mentioning banyans, the vertical

There is [also] a tree harder than all, which the strongest arrows can scarcely pierce.

12. The trees in this India, and also in India the Greater, never shed their leaves till the new ones come.[1]

13. To write about the other trees would be too long a business, and tedious beyond measure; seeing that they are many and divers, and beyond the comprehension of man.

14. But about wild beasts of the forest I say this: there be lions, leopards, ounces, and another kind something like a greyhound, having only the ears black and the whole body perfectly white, which among those people is called *Siagois*.[2] This animal, whatever it catches, never lets go, even to death. There is also another animal, which is called *Rhinoceros*,[3] as big as a horse, having one horn long and twisted; but it is not the *unicorn*.

15. There be also venomous animals, such as many serpents, big beyond bounds, and of divers colours, black, red,

shadow of which had a circumference of five hundred yards. Just about half this size is the largest I have seen, near Hushyárpúr in the Northern Punjab. It is remarkable in some of the largest of these trees, that you cannot tell which has been the original and "mother-tree," that having probably decayed and disappeared. The age of these trees is sometimes by no means so great as first impressions suggest. There is a very fine one in the Botanic Garden at Calcutta, (its exact size I do not remember, but the shade is not less than a hundred and eighty to two hundred feet across), whereof the garden tradition runs, that it originated in Roxburgh's time, *i.e.*, eighty or ninety years ago. It has, however, been carefully tended and *extended*, the vertical fibres being protected by bamboo tubes when young. It is said to have grown originally in the crown of a date tree, as often happens.

[1] True in a general way, but with exceptions, specific and local.

[2] *Siya-gosh* (black-ear), the Persian name of the lynx. I have not been able to hear of a *white* lynx. The lynx of the Dekkan, which is probably meant (*felis caracal*), has only the under part white, the back being a pale reddish brown. Its tenacity is a noted feature.

[3] "*Quod vocatur rinocerunta*"! The rhinoceros is not now, I believe, found in any part of India south (or west) of the Ganges; but it has become extinct in my own time in the forests of Rajmahl, on the right bank of that river; and very possibly extended at one time much further west, though our author's statement is too vague to build upon, and scarcely indicates personal knowledge of the animal.

white, and green, and parti-coloured; two-headed also, three-headed, and five-headed. Admirable marvels![1]

16. There be also coquodriles, which are vulgarly called *Calcatix*;[2] some of them be so big that they be bigger than the biggest horse. These animals be like lizards, and have a tail stretched over all, like unto a lizard's; and have a head like unto a swine's, and rows of teeth so powerful and horrible that no animal can escape their force, particularly in the water. This animal has, as it were, a coat of mail; and there is no sword, nor lance, nor arrow, which can anyhow hurt him, on account of the hardness of his scales. In the water, in short, there is nothing so strong, nothing so evil, as this wonderful animal. There be also many other reptiles, whose names, to speak plainly, I know not.

17. As for birds, I say plainly that they are of quite different kinds from what are found on this side of the world; except, indeed, crows and sparrows;[3] for there be parrots and popinjays in very great numbers, so that a thousand or more may be seen in a flock. These birds, when tamed and kept in cages, speak so that you would take them for rational beings. There be also bats really and truly as big as kites. These birds fly nowhither by day, but only when the sun sets. Wonderful! By day they hang themselves up on trees by the feet, with their bodies downwards, and in the daytime they look just like big fruit on the tree.[4]

[1] Two-headed and even three-headed serpents might be suggested by the portentous appearance of a cobra with dilated hood and spectacles, especially if the spectator were (as probably would be the case) in a great fright. But for *five* heads I can make no apology.

[2] This has puzzled me sorely, and I sought it vainly among Tamul and Malayalim synonyms. At the last moment the light breaks in upon me. It is, Fr., *cocatrix*; Ital., *calcatrice*; Anglicè, a *cockatrice*!

[3] Polo says: "Here and throughout all India the birds and beasts are different from ours, except one bird, which is the quail." (iii, 20.)

[4] A literally accurate description of the great Indian bat, or flying fox. They generally cluster on some great banyan tree. These, I presume, are what Marco Polo quaintly calls "bald owls which fly in the night: they have neither wings (?) nor feathers, and are as large as an eagle." (iii, 20.)

18. There are also other birds, such as peacocks, quails, Indian fowls,[1] and others, divers in kind; some white as white can be, some green as green can be, some parti-coloured, of such beauty as is past telling.

19. In this India, when men go to the wars, and when they act as guards to their lords, they go naked, with a round target,—a frail and paltry affair,—and holding a kind of a spit[2] in their hands; and, truly, their fighting seems like child's play.

20. In this India are many and divers precious stones, among which are the best diamonds under heaven. These stones never can be dressed or shaped by any art, except what nature has given. But I omit the properties of these stones, not to be prolix.

21. In this India are many other precious stones, endowed with excellent virtues, which may be gathered by anybody; nor is anyone hindered.

22. In this India, on the death of a noble, or of any people of substance, their bodies are burned: and eke their wives follow them alive to the fire, and, for the sake of worldly glory, and for the love of their husbands, and for eternal life, burn along with them, with as much joy as if they were going to be wedded; and those who do this have the higher repute for virtue and perfection among the rest.

There is a good account of the flying fox, and an excellent cut, in Tennent's *Nat. History of Ceylon*. On the Indiarubber trees at the Botanic Gardens near Kandy, they "hang in such prodigious numbers that frequently large branches give way beneath their accumulated weight." (p. 16.) Shall I be thought to be rivalling my author in the recital of marvels, if I say that in 1845 I saw, near Delhi, large branches which had been broken off by the accumulated weight—of *locusts* a few days before? So all the peasantry testified.

[1] Probably some kind of jungle-fowl, such as *Gallus Sonneratii*. Pheasants are not found in southern India.

[2] *Spatham*, a straight sword (?); but a contemptuous expression is evidently intended. Polo says: "The people go to battle with lance and shield, entirely naked; yet are they not valiant and courageous, but mean and cowardly."

Wonderful! I have sometimes seen, for one dead man who was burnt, five living women take their places on the fire with him, and die with their dead.

23. There be also other pagan-folk in this India who worship fire; they bury not their dead, neither do they burn them, but cast them into the midst of a certain roofless tower, and there expose them totally uncovered to the fowls of heaven. These believe in two First Principles, to wit, of Evil and of Good, of Darkness and of Light, matters which at present I do not purpose to discuss.[1]

24. There be also certain others which be called *Dumbri*, who eat carrion and carcases; who have absolutely no object of worship; and who have to do the drudgeries of other people, and carry loads.[2]

25. In this India there is green ginger, and it grows there in great abundance.[3]

There be also sugar-canes in quantities; carobs also, of such size and bigness that it is something stupendous.[4] I could tell very wonderful things of this India; but I am not able to detail them for lack of time. Cassia fistula is in some parts of this India extremely abundant.[5]

[1] Is not this short and accurate statement the first account of the Parsis in India, and of their strange disposal of the dead?

[2] The *Domra* or *Dōm*, one of the lowest Indian castes, and supposed to represent one of the aboriginal races. They are to this day, in Upper India, the persons generally employed to remove carcases, and to do the like jobs; sometimes also as hangmen. In the Dekkan they seem, according to Dubois (p. 468), who calls them *Dumbars*, to be often tumblers, conjurors, and the like.

[3] Ginger is cultivated in all parts of India. That of Malabar is best. (*Drury*.)

[4] *Carrobiæ*,—referring, I presume, to the carob of the Mediterranean (*Ceratonia siliqua*). I do not know what he means unless it be tamarinds, which are leguminous pods with some analogy to the carobs of the Mediterranean. The *trees* may often be called stupendous; but this seems scarcely to be his meaning. The European name is Arabic, *támar-ul-Hind* (date of India), as Linschoten long ago pointed out.

[5] *Cassia fistula* of Linnæus, if that be what is meant, is found in the Travancore forests, and probably all over India. Its beautiful, pendulous

26. The people of this India are very clean in their feeding; true in speech, and eminent in justice, maintaining carefully the privileges of every man according to his degree, as they have come down from old times.[1]

27. The heat there is perfectly horrible, and more intolerable to strangers than it is possible to say.[2]

racemes of yellow flowers, shewing something like a Brobdignag laburnum, make it a favourite in the gardens of Upper India. It affords a laxative medicine, and is given by Milburn among the exports of western India. The long, cylindrical pods, sometimes two feet long, probably give the specific name. It is possible, however, that the bishop did not mean *C. fistula*, but *cassia lignea*, an inferior cinnamon, which grows in Malabar forests, and was at one time largely exported from Calicut and the other ports. Barbosa mentions it as *canella selvatica*. Linschoten says that it was worth only about one-fifth of the Ceylon cinnamon. It is perhaps the cassia of Pliny. It is remarkable however that he says the choice cassia was called by the barbarians by the name of *lada*; and *lada* is the generic name which the Malays give to all the species of pepper, the word signifying *pungent*. (See *Drury*; *Crawfurd's Malay Dict.*; and *Bohn's Pliny*, xii, 43.)

[1] This is a remarkable testimony to the character of the Hindus when yet uninjured by foreign domination or much foreign intercourse. M. Polo says the Abraiamain (Brahmans) "are the best and most honest of all merchants, and would not on any account tell a lie" (p. 304). Rabbi Benjamin says also, "This nation is very trustworthy in matters of trade, and whenever foreign merchants enter their port, three secretaries of the king immediately repair on board their vessels, write down their names, and report them to him. The king thereupon grants them security for their property, which they may even leave in the open fields without any guard" (*Asher's Itinerary* of R. Benj. of Tud., p. 138 *et seq.*). There are many other passages, both in ancient and mediæval writers, giving an extravagantly high character for integrity and veracity to the Hindus, a character not very often deserved by them, and never ascribed to them, now-a-days. See some remarks on this subject in *Elphinstone's History*, book iii. ch. xi.

It is curious, however, that, with reference to the very district of Travancore, which now includes Quilon, where the bishop's experience must have chiefly lain, two English Residents have borne testimony lamentably opposed to his account of the character of the people in former times. One of these declares that "he never knew a people so destitute of truth and honesty, or so abandoned to vice and corruption"; the other asserts that "in no part of the world are men to be found to whose habits and affections the practice of vice is so familiar" (*Hamilton's Desc. Hindost.*, ii. 315).

[2] Says Marco, "The heat of the sun can scarcely be endured; if you

28. In this India there exists not, nor is found, any metal but what comes from abroad, except gold, iron, and electrum. There is no pepper there, nor any kind of spice except ginger.

29. In this India the greater part of the people worship idols, although a great share of the sovereignty is in the hands of the Turkish Saracens, who came forth from Multan, and conquered and usurped dominion to themselves not long since, and destroyed an infinity of idol temples, and likewise many churches, of which they made mosques for Mahomet, taking possession of their endowments and property. 'Tis grief to hear, and woe to see![1]

30. The Pagans of this India have prophecies of their own that we Latins are to subjugate the whole world.[2]

31. In this India there is a scattered people, one here, another there, who call themselves Christians, but are not so, nor have they baptism, nor do they know anything else about the faith. Nay, they believe St. Thomas the Great to be Christ!

32. There, in the India I speak of, I baptized and brought into the faith about three hundred souls, of whom many were idolaters and Saracens.[3]

put an egg into any river, it will be boiled before you have gone any great distance." (iii. 25.)

[1] The reason of the reference to Multán is obscure. The allusion would seem to be to the conquest of the Carnatic and Malabar by the generals of the Khilji sovereigns of Delhi, Alá-ud-din and Mubárik (A.D. 1310—1319). The Khiljis were Turks by descent. Mooltan was at this time subject to Delhi (*Elphinstone's History*, pp. 343, 348, and *Briggs's Ferishta*). But, perhaps, the "not long since" has a wider import, and refers to the conquests and iconoclasms of the great Mahmúd of Ghazni, 300 years before. Indeed, he is here speaking of the Lesser India, *i.e.* of Sindh, Gujerat, and the Konkan, the scene of some of Mahmúd's most memorable expeditions. Mahmúd coming from Ghazni would come *through* Multán, and indeed he took that city several times.

[2] Perhaps a reference to the notions of Mahomedans about the latter days. But I think I have read of indications of this belief among Hindus, though I cannot quote them. This one is remarkable at so early a date.

[3] I need scarcely say that by Saracens he means Mahomedans, just as

33. And let me tell you that among the idolaters a man may with safety expound the Word of the Lord; nor is anyone from among the idolaters hindered from being baptized throughout all the East, whether they be Tartars, or Indians, or what not.

34. These idolaters sacrifice to their gods in this manner; to wit, there is one man who is priest to the idol, and he wears a long shirt, down to the ground almost, and above this a white surplice[1] in our fashion; and he has a clerk with a shirt who goes after him, and carries a hassock, which he sets before the priest. And upon this the priest kneels, and so begins to advance from a distance, like one performing his stations; and he carries upon his bent arms a tray of two cubits [long], all full of eatables of different sorts, with lighted tapers at top; and thus praying he comes up to the altar where the idol is, and deposits the offering before it after their manner; and he pours a libation, and places part [of the offering] in the hands of the idol, and then divides the residue, and himself eats a part of it.

35. They make idols after the likeness of almost all living things of the idolaters; and they have besides their god according to his likeness.[2] It is true that over all gods they place One God, the Almighty Creator of all those.[3] They

these were called *Moors* by our people in India in the last century, and by some classes of Europeans perhaps to our own day. So also the Prayer-book, in the collect for Good Friday, speaks of "Jews, TURKS, infidels, and heretics."

1 "*Planeta.*"

2 Somewhat obscure. "*Isti faciunt idola ferè ad similitudinem omnium rerum idolotrarum animantium; habent desuper deum suum, ad similitudinem suam.*"

3 Apart from the Brahminical theosophies, the expressions of Hindus generally, when *religious* (not superstitious) feeling or expression is drawn out, by sorrow or the like, are often purely Theistic. *Parmeswar* or *Bhagwán* in such cases is evidently meant to express the One Almighty, and no fabled divinity. But the old geographer in Ramusio makes the singular assertion that "all the country of Malabar believes in the Trinity, Father, Son, and Holy Spirit, and this beginning at Cambay and ending

hold also that the world has existed now xxviii thousand years.[1]

The Indians, both of this India and of the other Indies, never kill an ox, but rather honour him like a father; and some, even perhaps the majority, worship him. They will more readily spare him who has slain five men than him who has slain one ox, saying that it is no more lawful to kill an ox than to kill one's father. This is because oxen do all their services, and moreover furnish them with milk and butter, and all sorts of good things.[2] The great lords among the idolaters, every morning when they rise, and before they go anywhither, make the fattest cows come before them, and lay their hands upon them, and then rub their own faces, believing that after this they can have no ailment.

36. Let this be enough about Lesser India; for were I to set forth particulars of everything down to worms and the like, a year would not suffice for the description.

37. But [I may say in conclusion] as for the women and men, the blacker they be, the more beautiful they be [held.][3]

at Bengal". Conti says the same at Ava, but *he* was doubtless misled by the Buddhist triad, *Buddha, Dharma, Sangha*—the Divine person, the Law, and the Congregation.

[1] This does not agree in any way with any version of the Hindu mythical chronology that I know of.

[2] It would go hard with a man yet in a Hindu state who should kill an ox. It was capital under the Sikhs.

[3] "Whoever is most deeply tinted is honoured in proportion" (*M. Polo*, p. 304). So, among the flat-nosed Mongols, Rubruquis says, "*et quæ minus habet de naso, illa pulchrior reputatur!*"

V.

HERE FOLLOWETH CONCERNING INDIA THE GREATER.

1. Of India the Greater I say this; that it is like unto Lesser India as regards all the folk being black. The animals also are all similar, neither more nor less [in number], except elephants, which they have [in the former] in very great plenty. These animals are marvellous; for they exceed in size and bulk and strength, and also in understanding, all the animals of the world. This animal hath a big head; small eyes, smaller than a horse's; ears like the wings of owls or bats; a nose reaching quite to the ground, extending right down from the top of his head; and two tusks standing out of remarkable magnitude [both in] bulk and length, which are [in fact] teeth rooted in the upper jaw. This animal doth everything by word of command; so that his driver hath nothing to do but say once, "Do this," and he doeth it; nor doth he seem in other respects a brute, but rather a rational creature. They have very big feet, with six hoofs like those of an ox, or rather of a camel.[1] This animal carrieth easily upon him, with a certain structure of timber, more than thirty men; and he is a most gentle beast,[2] and trained for war, so that a single animal counteth by himself equal in war to 1,500 men and more; for they bind to his tusks blades or maces of iron wherewith he smiteth. Most horrible are the powers of this beast, and specially in war.

2. Two things there be which cannot be withstood by arms: one is the bolt of heaven; the second is a stone from

[1] Than the bishop's description thus far I doubt if a better is to be found till long after his time. The numbers of men represented to be carried on the *hauda* seem not very credible to us and must be exaggerated, but all ancient accounts do speak of much larger numbers than we now-a-days are accustomed to put upon elephants under any circumstances.

[2] "A very pious animal," as a German friend in India said to me, misled by the double sense of his vernacular *fromm*.

an artillery engine; this is a third! For there is nothing that either can or dare stand against the assault of an elephant in any manner. A marvellous thing! He kneeleth, lieth, sitteth, goeth and cometh, merely at his master's word. In short, it is impossible to write in words the peculiarities of this animal.

3. In this India there are pepper and ginger, cinnamon, brazil,[1] and all other spices.

4. Ginger is the root of a plant which hath leaves like a reed. Pepper is the fruit of a plant something like ivy, which climbs trees, and forms grape-like fruit like that of the wild vine.[2] This fruit is at first green, then when it comes to maturity it becomes all black and corrugated as you see it. 'Tis thus that long pepper is produced, nor are you to believe that fire is placed under the pepper, nor that it is roasted, as some will lyingly maintain.[3] Cinnamon is

[1] *Brazil.* This is the sappan-wood, affording a red dye, from a species of *caesalpina* found in nearly all tropical Asia, from Malabar eastward. The name of brazil wood is now appropriated to that (derived from another species of caesalpina) which comes from Brazil, and which, according to Macculloch, gives twice as much dye from the same weight of wood. The history of the names here is worthy of note. First, *brazil* is the name of the Indian wood in commerce. Then the great country is called *Brazil*, because a somewhat similar wood is found abundantly there. And now the Indian wood is robbed of its name, which is appropriated to that found in a country of the New World, and is supposed popularly to be derived from the name of that country. I do not know the origin of the word *brazil*. Sappan is from the Malay name *(sapang)*.

[2] "*Lambruscæ.*"

[3] The black pepper vine is indigenous in the forests of Malabar and Travancore (the districts which the Bishop has in his eye); and the Malabar pepper is acknowledged to be the best that is produced. The vines are planted at the base of trees with rough bark, the mango and others, and will climb twenty or thirty feet if allowed. After being gathered, the berries are dried on mats in the sun, turning from red to black. Pepper was for ages *the* staple article of export to Europe from India, and it was with it that Vasco de Gama loaded his ships on his first voyage. A very interesting article on pepper will be found in that treasury of knowledge, Crawfurd's *Dictionary of the Archipelago.*

The Bishop's mention of "long pepper" shews confusion, probably in his amanuensis or copyist; for long pepper is the produce of a different

the bark of a large tree which has fruit and flowers like cloves.[1]

5. In this India be many islands, and more than 10,000 of them inhabited, as I have heard; wherein are many world's wonders.[2] For there is one called Silem, where are found the best precious stones in the whole world, and in the greatest quantity and number, and of all kinds.[3]

6. Between that island and the main are taken pearls or marguerites, in such quantity as to be quite wonderful. So indeed that there are sometimes more than 8,000 boats or vessels, for three months continuously, [engaged in this fishery]. It is astounding, and almost incredible, to those who have not seen it, how many are taken.

7. Of birds I say this: that there be many different from

genus *(Chavica)*, which is *not* a vine, but a shrub, whose stems are annual. The chemical composition and properties are nearly the same as those of black pepper. Crawfurd draws attention to the fact that, by Pliny's account, *piper longum* bore between three and four times the price of black pepper in the Roman market. *(Drury* in voc.—*Crawfurd's Dict.)* Though long pepper is now cultivated in Malabar, it was not so, or at least not *exported*, in the sixteenth century. Linschoten says expressly that the "long pepper groweth onely in Bengala and Java." (p. 111.) Its price at Rome was probably therefore a fancy one, due to its rarity. It is curious that Pliny supposed pepper to grow in pods, and that the long pepper was the immature pod picked and prepared for the market. He corrects a popular error that ginger was the root of the pepper tree (bk. xii). Ibn Batuta, like our Bishop, contradicts what "some have said, that they boil it in order to dry it," as without foundation. But their predecessor, R. Benjamin, says—"the pepper is originally white, but when they collect it, they put it in basins and pour hot water upon it; it is then exposed to the heat of the sun," etc.

[1] The cinnamon must have been the wild cinnamon or cassia. There is an article in Indian commerce called "cassia buds," bearing some resemblance to cloves, and having the flavour of cinnamon. It is said by some to be the unexpanded flower of the Laurus cassia, but, strange to say, this seems still undetermined. (See *Penny Cyc.*)

[2] Polo says the islands of India are estimated at 12,700 inhabited and uninhabited (iii, 37), and those of the China Sea at 7,448 (iii, 5). The Lakkadives are supposed to derive their name from Laksha or Lakh = 100,000.

[3] Ceylon, called by Polo Seilan, and the same by Ibn Batuta.

those of Lesser India, and of different colours; for there be some white all over as snow; some red as scarlet of the grain; some green as grass; some parti-coloured; in such quantity and delectability as cannot be uttered. Parrots also, or popinjays, after their kind, of every possible colour except black, for black ones are never found; but white all over, and green, and red, and also of mixed colours. The birds of this India seem really like creatures of Paradise.[1]

8. There is also told a marvellous thing of the islands aforesaid, to wit that there is one of them in which there is a water, and a certain tree in the middle of it. Every metal which is washed with that water becomes gold; every wound on which are placed the bruised leaves of that tree is incontinently healed.

9. In this India, whilst I was at Columbum, were found two cats having wings like the wings of bats;[2] and in Lesser India there be some rats as big as foxes, and venomous exceedingly.[3]

10. In this India are certain trees which have leaves so

[1] The gorgeous lories of the Archipelago must have been imported to Quilon, and have been here in the Bishop's remembrance.

[2] No doubt the large flying squirrel, which is found in Malabar and Ceylon as well as in Eastern India.

[3] The bandicoot; *Mus Malabaricus,* or *Mus giganticus.* The name is said by Sir E. Tennent (*Nat. Hist. of Ceylon,* p. 44) to be from the Teloogoo *Pandi-koku,* "Pig-rat." "This rat is found in many places on the coast of Coromandel, in Mysore, and in several parts of Bengal between Calcutta and Hurdwar. It is a most mischievous animal, burrows to a great depth, and will pass under the foundations of granaries and storehouses if not carefully laid." (*General Hardwicke* in *Linnæan Trans.,* vii., quoted in *Pen. Cyc.,* article *Muridæ.*) The animal figured by Hardwicke was a female; its total length was 26¼ inches, of which the tail was 13 inches; and the weight was 2 pounds 11½ ounces. This is not quite so big as a fox, though the foxes in India *are* very small. As an exaggeration, it is far from a parallel to that of Herodotus, who speaks (bk. iii.) of *ants* in India as big as foxes. A story which reminds one of the question of a young Scotch lady just arrived in the Hoogly, when she saw an elephant for the first time, "Wull yon be what's called a *musqueetae?*"

big that five or six men can very well stand under the shade of one of them.[1]

11. In the aforesaid island of Sylen is a very potent king, who hath precious stones of every kind under heaven, in such quantity as to be almost incredible. Among these he hath two rubies, of which he weareth one hung round his neck, and the other on the hand wherewith he wipeth his lips and his beard ; and [each] is of greater length than the breadth of four fingers, and when held in the hand it standeth out visibly on either side to the breadth of a finger. I do not believe that the universal world hath two stones like these, or of so great a price, of the same species.[2]

12. There is also another island where all the men and women go absolutely naked, and have in place of money comminuted gold like fine sand. They make of the cloth which they buy walls like curtains ;[3] nor do they cover themselves or their shame at any time in the world.

13. There is also another exceeding great island, which is called Jaua,[4] which is in circuit more than seven [thousand ?] miles as I have heard,[5] and where are many world's wonders. Among which, besides the finest aromatic spices, this is one, to wit, that there be found pygmy men, of the

[1] The Talipat (*Corypha umbraculifera*), or great fan-palm, abundant in Ceylon, and found in the southern part of the peninsula, in Burma, and in the Malay islands, but scarcely known in Bengal. The leaves, according to Sir J. E. Tennent, have sometimes an area of two hundred square feet.

[2] "The King [of Ceylon] has the most beautiful ruby that ever was or can be in the whole world. It is the most splendid object on earth, and seems to glow like fire ; it is of such value as money could scarcely purchase." (*Polo*, iii. 17).

"I also saw in the possession of the King [of Ceylon] a saucer made of ruby, as large as the palm of the hand, in which he kept oil of aloes. I was much surprised at it, when the king said to me, 'We have much larger than this.'" (*Ibn Batuta*, p. 187).

[3] "*De pannis quos emunt faciunt ad modum cortinarum parietes.*"

[4] "*Jana,*" by mistranscription doubtless.

[5] His Java vaguely represents the Archipelago generally, with some special reference to Sumatra.

size of a boy of three or four years old, all shaggy like a he goat. They dwell in the woods, and few are found.[1]

14. In this island also are white mice, exceeding beautiful. There also are trees producing cloves, which, when they are in flower, emit an odour so pungent that they kill every man who cometh among them, unless he shut his mouth and nostrils.[2]

15. There too are produced cubebs, and nutmegs, and mace, and all the other finest spices except pepper.[3]

16. In a certain part of that island they delight to eat white and fat men when they can get them.[4]

17. In the Greater India, and in the islands, all the people

[1] Polo, in one chapter on Sumatra, tells how stuffed pygmies were manufactured for the western markets by shaving monkeys, "for neither in India, nor in any other country however savage, are there men so small as these pretended ones." Yet, in another chapter, his incredulity gives way, and he tells of hairy men with tails, who remain in the mountains, never visiting the towns. No doubt the orang-utang, which exists in Sumatra, is at the bottom of these pygmy stories. The pygmies and cannibals together identify Sumatra as the scene of one of Sindbad's adventures; not the Andamans, as a reviewer in the *Athenæum* lately said.

[2] This seems to be a jumble of the myths about the spice-groves and the upas tree.

[3] The cubeb (*Piper cubeba* and *P. caricum*) is the only one of the spices named which grows in Java proper. In those days it was probably exported as a condiment chiefly. This statement that pepper was not produced in the islands confirms the inference of the sagacious Crawfurd, that it is exotic in Sumatra. (See his *Dict. of the Archip.*, article *Pepper.*)

[4] In Sumatra, we read, "Man's flesh, if it be fat, is eaten as ordinarily there as beefe in our country. Marchants comming vnto this region for traffique do vsually bring to them fat men, selling them vnto the inhabitants as we sel hogs, who immediately kil and eate them." (*Odoricus*, in Hakluyt, vol. ii.)

"In one part of the island, called *Batech*, the inhabitants eat human flesh," etc. (*Conti* in *India in the Fifteenth Century*, p. 9.) The cannibalism of certain tribes in Sumatra is noticed with more or less exaggeration by several other old travellers, and has been confirmed in the present century. The tribe is that of the Battas or Battaks, as correctly named by Conti, a race presenting the singular anomaly of Anthropophagi with a literature. Some have supposed that they may be the cannibal *Paddaei* of Herodotus (iii. 99). It is not impossible, for the more we learn the further goes back the history of Eastern navigation.

4

be black, and go naked from the loins upwards, and from the knee downwards, and without shoes.

18. But the kings have this distinction from others, that they wear upon their arms gold and silver rings, and on the neck a gold collar with a great abundance of gems.[1]

19. In this India never do [even] the legitimate sons of great kings, or princes, or barons, inherit the goods of their parents, but only the sons of their sisters; for they say that they have no surety that those are their own sons, because wives and mistresses may conceive and generate by some one else; but 'tis not so with the sister, for whatever man may be the father they are certain that the offspring is from the womb of their sister, and is consequently thus truly of their blood.[2]

20. In this Greater India many sacrifice themselves to idols in this way. When they are sick, or involved in any grave mischance, they vow themselves to the idol if they should happen to be delivered. Then, when they have recovered, they fatten themselves for one or two years continually, eating and drinking fat things, etc. And when another

[1] "Now, in all this province of Maabar, there is not a tailor, for the people go naked at every season. The air is always so temperate, that they wear only a piece of cloth round the middle. The king is dressed just like the others, except that his cloth is finer, and he wears a necklace full set with rubies, etc. He wears also round three parts both of his arms and legs, bracelets of gold, full of goodly stones and pearls." (*Polo*, iii. 20.)

[2] For the continued existence of this remarkable custom of inheritance among the Nairs of Malabar, and for a description of the singular relations of the sexes out of which it springs, see a statement in Mr. Markham's late *Travels in Peru and India*, p. 345. I am collecting, for another paper, the various examples of this law of inheritance in detail, and will only here mention that it exists, or has existed, also in Canara, (but there derived from the Nairs); among the aborigines of Hispaniola, and tribes of New Granada and Bogota; among negro tribes of the Niger; among certain sections of the Malays of Sumatra; in the royal family of Tipura, and among the Kasias of the Sylhet mountains (both east of Bengal); in a district of Ceylon adjoining Bintenne; in Madagascar; in the Fiji islands; and among the Hurons and Natchez of North America.

festival comes round, they cover themselves with flowers and perfumes, and crown themselves with white garlands, and go with singing and playing before the idol when it is carried through the land (like the image of the Virgin Mary here among us at the Rogation tides); and those men who are sacrificing themselves to the idol carry a sword with two handles, like those [knives] which are used in currying leather; and, after they have shown off a great deal, they put the sword to the back of the neck, cutting strongly with a vigorous exertion of both hands, and so cut off their own heads before the idol.[1]

[1] Barbosa says that the King of Quilacare (Coilacaud), a city near Cape Comorin, after reigning twelve years, always sacrificed himself to an idol. See also *Odoricus*, in Hakluyt, ii. 161. The singular narrative in the text reminds us of Sir Jonah Barrington's story of the Irish mower, who, making a dig at a salmon in a pool with the butt end of his scythe, which was over his shoulder, dropt his own head into the water. There is a remarkably parallel story in *Ibn Batuta*. When he was at the court of the pagan king of Mul-Java (which is certainly not Java, as the editors make it, but, as I hope to show elsewhere, Cambodia, or some country on the main in that quarter), he says, "I one day saw, in the assembly of this prince, a man with a long knife in his hand, which he placed upon his own neck; he then made a long speech, not a word of which I could understand; he then firmly grasped the knife, and its sharpness, and the force with which he urged it, were such that he severed his head from his body, and it fell on the ground. I was wondering much at the circumstance, when the king said to me: 'Does any one among you do such a thing as this?' I answered, 'I never saw one do so.' He smiled, and said: 'These, our servants, do so out of their love to us.' One who had been present at the assembly, told me that the speech he made was a declaration of his love to the sultan, and that on this account he had killed himself, just as his father had done for the father of the present king, and his grandfather for the king's grandfather." (*Lee's Ibn Batuta*, p. 205.) Also we are told by Abu Zaid al Hasan, in Reinaud's *Relation des Voyages faits par les Arabes*, etc. (Paris, 1845), how a young man of India, tying his hair to a great elastic bamboo stem, which was pulled down to the ground, cut his own head off, telling his friends to watch that they might see and hear how the head would *laugh*, as it sprung aloft with the resilient bamboo (i. 124). I wish I could relate, with the interesting detail with which it was told to me, a narrative which I heard from my friend Lieut.-Colonel Keatinge, V.C., of the Bombay Artillery. When encamped near a certain sacred rock on the Nerbudda, in the province of Nimar which was under his charge, a stalwart young man was

21. In this Greater India, in the place where I was, the nights and days are almost equal, nor does one exceed the other in length at any season by so much as a full hour.

22. In this India the sun keeps to the south for six months continuously, casting the shadows to the north; and for the other six months keeps to the north, casting the shadow to the south.[1]

23. In this India the Pole-star is seen very low, insomuch that I was at one place where it did not show above the earth or the sea more than two fingers' breadth.[2]

24. There the nights, when the weather is fine and there is no moon, are, if I err not, four times as clear as in our part of the world.

25. There also, if I err not, between evening and morning, often all the planets may be seen; there are seen their influences [as it were] eye to eye, so that 'tis a delightful thing there to look out at night![3]

26. From the place aforesaid is seen continually between the south and the east a star of great size and ruddy splendour, which is called Canopus, and which from these parts of the world is never visible.

brought to him, who had come thither from a distance, for the purpose of sacrificing himself by casting himself from the cliff, in fulfilment of a vow made by his own mother before his birth, in case she should, after long sterility, have a living son. After long remonstrance Colonel Keatinge at last succeeded in convincing him that it would be quite lawful to sacrifice a goat instead, and this having been done he departed with a relieved mind.

[1] As Quilon is between 8° and 9° of north latitude this is somewhat overstated.

[2] So Polo says that at Guzerat "the north star rose to the apparent height of six cubits". This way of estimating celestial declinations appears to convey some distinct meaning to simple people, and even to some by no means illiterate Europeans. I remember once in India, when looking out for Venus, which was visible about two p.m., a native servant directed me to look "about one bamboo length from the moon;" and a young Englishman afterwards told me that he had seen it "about five feet from the moon."

[3] "*Ibi videntur influentiæ oculo ad oculum, ita quod de nocte respicere est gaudiosum.*"

27. There are many marvellous things in the cycle of those [heavenly bodies] to delight a good astronomer.[1]

28. In this India, and in India the Less, men who dwell a long way from the sea, under the ground and in woody tracts, seem altogether infernal; neither eating, drinking, nor clothing themselves like the others who dwell by the sea.[2]

29. There serpents too be numerous, and very big, of all colours in the world; and it is a great marvel that they be seldom or never found to hurt anybody unless first attacked.

30. There is there also a certain kind of wasps, which make it their business to kill very big spiders whenever they find them, and afterwards to bury them in the sand, in a

[1] "*Astrologo.*"

[2] Perhaps the good bishop by *infernales* does not mean *infernal,* but only *inferior.* Yet the expression reminds us of the constant strain of oriental tradition, which represents the aborigines under the aspect of *Rakshasas* or Demons. The reference is to the various forest tribes of the Peninsula, who represent either the Dravidian races unmodified by civilization, (whether Hindu or pre-Hindu), or some yet antecedent races. Dubois, speaking generally of the wild forest tribes of the south, says, "In the rainy season they shelter themselves in caverns, hollow trees, and clefts of the rocks; and in fine weather they keep the open field. They are almost entirely naked. The women wear nothing to conceal their nakedness but some leaves of trees stitched together, and bound round their waists," etc. (473.) And Mr. Markham describes the Poliars, a race of wild and timid men of the woods in the Pulney Hills, east of Cochin, who are possibly the very people whom Jordanus had in his eye, as being said to have no habitations, but to run through the jungle from place to place, to sleep under rocks, and live on wild honey and roots. They occasionally trade with the peasantry, who place cotton and grain on some stone, and the wild creatures, as soon as the strangers are out of sight, take these and put honey in their place. But they will let no one come near them. (*Peru and India,* p. 404.) These wild races were no doubt in the mind's eye of a little Hindu, who, during the examination of a native school by a late governor of Madras (now again occupying an eminent position in India), on being asked what became of the original inhabitants of Britain at the Saxon conquest? replied, "They fled into Wales and *Cornwall,* and other remote parts, where they exist as a wild and barbarous people to this day!" The little Hindu was not aware that—

"By Pol, *Tre,* and Pen
You may know the Cornish men."

deep hole which they make, and so to cover them up that there is no man in the world who can turn them up, or find the place.[1]

31. There is also a kind of very small ants, white as wool, which have such hard teeth that they gnaw through even timbers and the joints of stones,[2] and, in short, whatever dry thing they find on the face of the earth, and mutilate woollen and cotton clothes. And they build out of the finest sand a crust like a wall, so that the sun cannot reach them, and s they remain covered. But if that crust happens to get broken, so that the sun reaches them, they incontinently die.[3]

32. As regards insects, there be wonders, so many, great, and marvellous, that they cannot be told.

33. There is also in this India a certain bird, big like a kite, having a white head and belly, but all red above, which boldly snatches fish out of the hands of fishermen and other people, and indeed [these birds] go on just like dogs.[4]

[1] This is the practice of certain solitary wasps and kindred species, both in Europe and India (see *Kirby and Spence,* Letter xi., etc.). The spiders, etc., form a store of food for the use of the larvæ when hatched.

[2] "*Venas lapidum.*"

[3] The most remarkable operation of white ants that I have heard of was told me by a scientific man, and I believe may be depended on. Having a case of new English harness, which he was anxious to secure from the white ants, he moved it about six inches from the wall, and placed it on stone vessels filled with water (as is often done), so that he considered it quite isolated and safe. On opening the case some time after he found the harness ruined, and on looking behind he saw that the white ants had actually projected their "crust" across the gap from the wall, so as to reach their prey by a tubular bridge. Here is engineering design as well as execution! The ants have apparently a great objection to working under the light of day, but that they "incontinently die" is a mistake.

[4] ? "*Et sic se ingerunt sicut canes.*" This appears to refer to the common rufous kite, abundant all over India. Of this, or a kindred kite, Sir J. E. Tennent says, "The ignoble birds of prey, the kites, keep close by the shore, and hover round the returning boats of the fishermen, to feast on the fry rejected from the nets" (*Nat. Hist. of C.*, p. 246) The action described in the text is quite that of the Indian kite. I recollect seeing one

34. There is also another big bird, not like a kite, which flies only at night, and utters a voice in the night season like the voice of a man wailing from the deep.[1]

35. What shall I say then? Even the Devil too there speaketh to men, many a time and oft, in the night season, as I have heard.[2]

36. Every thing indeed is a marvel in this India! Verily it is quite another world!

37. There is also a certain part of that India which is called Champa. There, in place of horses, mules and asses, and camels, they make use of elephants for all their work.[3]

swoop down upon a plate, which a servant was removing from the breakfast table in camp, and carry off the top of a silver muffineer, which however it speedily dropped.

[1] This may be the bird spoken of in the latter part of the next note, but I think it is probably the *Kulang* (of Bengal), or great crane (*Grus cinerea*), which does travel at night, with a wailing cry during its flight.

[2] "*Ut ego audivi.*" Ambiguum est, an ipse episcopus D——m loquentem audivisset? Not many years ago, an eccentric gentleman wrote from Sikkim to the secretary of the Asiatic Society in Calcutta, stating that, on the snows of the mountains there, were found certain mysterious footsteps, *more than thirty or forty paces asunder*, which the natives alleged to be *Shaitan's*. The writer at the same time offered, if Government would give him leave of absence for a certain period, etc., to go and trace the author of these mysterious vestiges, and thus this strange creature would be discovered *without any expense to Government*. The notion of catching Shaitan without any expense to Government was a sublime piece of Anglo-Indian tact, but the offer was not accepted. Our author had, however, in view probably the strange cry of the Devil-bird, as it is called in Ceylon. "The Singhalese regard it literally with horror, and its scream by night in the vicinity of a village is bewailed as the harbinger of impending calamity." "Its ordinary note is a magnificent clear shout, like that of a human being, and which can be heard at a great distance, and has a fine effect in the silence of the closing night. It has another cry like that of a hen just caught; but the sounds which have earned for it its bad name, and which I have heard but once to perfection, are indescribable, the most appalling that can be imagined, and scarcely to be heard without shuddering; I can only compare it to a boy in torture, whose screams are stopped by being strangled." Mr. Mitford, from whom Sir E. Tennent quotes the last passage, considers it to be a *Podargus* or night-hawk, rather than the brown owl as others have supposed. (*Tennent's Nat. Hist. of Ceylon*, 246-8.)

[3] Champa is the Malay name of the coast of Cambodia, and appears in

38. 'Tis a wonderful thing about these animals, that when they are in a wild state they challenge each other to war, and form troops [for the purpose]; so that there will be sometimes a hundred against a hundred, more or less; and they put the strongest and biggest and boldest at the head, and thus attack each other in turn, so that within a short time there will remain in one place XL or L killed and wounded, more or less. And 'tis a notable thing that the vanquished, it is said, never again appear in war or in the field.

39. These animals, on account of their ivory, are worth as much dead as alive, nor are they ever taken when little, but only when big and full grown.

40. And the mode of taking them is wonderful. Enclosures are made, very strong, and of four sides, wherein be many gateways, and raised gates, formed of very big and strong timbers. And there is one trained female elephant which is taken near the place where the elephants come to feed. The one which they desire to catch is pointed out to her, and she is told to manage so as to bring him home. She goeth about him and about him, and so contriveth by stroking him and licking him, as to induce him to follow her, and to enter along with her the outer gate, which the keepers incontinently let fall. Then, when the wild elephant turneth about, the female entereth the second gate, which is instantly shut like the first, and so the [wild] elephant remaineth caught between the two gates. Then cometh a man, clothed in black or red, with his face covered, who cruelly thrasheth him from above, and crieth out abusively against him as against a thief; and this goeth on for five or six days, without his getting anything to eat or drink. Then cometh

some form in our maps. Jordanus may have derived his information about those countries from his brother friar, Odoricus, who visited Champa, and mentions the king's having 10,004 elephants. Late travellers in Cambodia use almost the expression in the text in speaking of the habitual employment of elephants in that country (*e. g.*, see Mr. King, in *Jour. Geog. Soc.* for 1860, p. 178).

another fellow, with his face bare, and clad in another colour, who feigneth to smite the first man, and to drive and thrust him away; then he cometh to the elephant and talketh to him, and with a long spear he scratcheth him, and he kisseth him, and giveth him food; and this goeth on for ten or fifteen days, and so by degrees he ventureth down beside him, and bindeth him to another elephant. And thus, after about twenty days, he may be taken out to be taught and broken in.[1]

41. In this Greater India are twelve idolatrous kings, and more.[2] For there is one very powerful king in the country

[1] This is evidently drawn from the life. Compare the account of elephant taming in Burma in the *Mission to Ava in* 1855, pp. 103-5, and the authors there quoted.

[2] The number *twelve* is only general and conventional. Ibn Batuta says there were twelve kings in Malabar alone, and even a greater number are alluded to by some of the old travellers. It is extremely difficult to trace these kingdoms, both from the looseness of the statements and want of accessible histories of the states of Southern India, and from that absence of any distinction between really substantial monarchies and mere principalities of small account, which may be noticed in Polo and the other travellers of the time as well as in our author.

Telenc, however, he speaks of as a potent and great kingdom. This must have been the kingdom of interior Telingana, called *Andra*, the capital of which was Warangól, eighty miles north-east of Hyderabad, and which was powerful and extensive at the end of the thirteenth century. It was shortly afterwards invaded by the armies of the king of Delhi; the capital was taken in 1332, and the sovereignty at a later date merged in the Mussulman kingdom of Golkonda.

There does not seem to have been any very great kingdom in the Mahratta country at this time, and perhaps this is the reason why he there speaks of the kingdom, not of the king. The most powerful princes were the rajas of Deogiri (afterwards Daulutabad), of the Yadu family. Their dynasty was subverted by the Mahommedans in 1317. I believe there is no mention of the Mahrattas by the Mussulman historians till just about our author's time.

Columbum, or Kulam, we have disposed of in the preface. We see here that the kingdom included (part at least of) Mohebar, the Maabar of Marco Polo and of Ibn Batuta, *i.e.*, the southern regions of the Coromandel coast; (see Preface, p. xvi). The name is apparently Arabic (*Ma'abar*—a ferry), in reference to the passage or ferry to Ceylon. The king, whose name was *Lingua*, may probably have been connected with the sect of the *Lingáyets* still existing in Southern India, whose members wear a representation of

where pepper grows, and his kingdom is called Molebar. There is also the king of Singuyli and the king of Columbum,

the Lingam or Sivaite emblem round their necks, and have many peculiar practices. He was certainly a Nair, as appears from what Jordanus has said of the law of succession. And among the rajas of Coorg, who were both Nairs and Lingayets, we find the name Linga borne by several during the last century. (Compare *Markham's Peru and India; Hamilton's Hindostan*, ii. 288, etc.)

I cannot trace any particulars of a king of Molepoor or Molepatam. But the only pearl fishery on the Indian main is at *Tuticorin,* about ninety miles north-east of Cape Comorin, and near this there is a place given by Hamilton, called Mooloopetta (= Mooloopatam), which may probably be the seat of the king alluded to. He was most likely the same as the king of Cail, spoken of by Marco Polo; that place being apparently now represented by Coilpatam, a small seaport of Tinnevelly, in this immediate vicinity. This appears from Barbosa, who, at the beginning of the sixteenth century, states precisely that Cail was ninety miles from Cape Comorin, and that it was the seat of a great pearl market and fishery.

Batigala, or Batikala, which, he says, had a Saracen king, is a port of Canara, fifty-five miles north of Mangalore; it is called Batcul, or Batcole, in English maps. It is not mentioned by Ibn Batuta, the nearest authority in time; but he does state that at Hinaur (Hunawur or Onore), a port a little to the north of Baticala, the people were Moslem, and their king "one of the best of princes," one *Jamál ad-Dín Mahommed Ibn Hasan,* to whom Malabar generally paid tribute, dreading his bravery by sea, (which means, I suppose, that this excellent prince was a pirate). Very probably this was the king of Batigala to whom Jordanus refers. He was, however, himself "subject to an infidel king, whose name was Horaib" (*Lee's Ibn Batuta,* p. 166), doubtless the king of Narsinga or Bisnagur, whom Jordanus omits to mention. Two centuries later Barbosa describes Batticala as a great place, where many merchants trafficked, and where were many *Moors* and Gentiles, great merchants. And the "*Summary of Kingdoms,*" in *Ramusio*, says the king of Baticula was then a Gentile Canarese, "greater than him of Honor;" the governor, however, being a Moorish eunuch, named Caipha. Later in the sixteenth century, Vincent Le Blanc describes it as still a fine place, and one of great trade.

The great king of Molebar, or Malabar, is, I suppose, the Samudra Raja, or Zamorin of the Portuguese, whose capital was at Calicut.

Singuyli is a nut hard to crack. Our friar's contemporary, Odoricus, calls the two chief ports of the pepper country in his day *Flandrina* and *Cyncilim*. The former is no doubt the *Fandaraina* of Ibn Batuta, "a large and beautiful place," the Colam Pandarani of Ramusio's Geographer, lying a little north of Calicut, but not marked in our modern maps. (The lying Mandevill says it was called Flandrina after Flanders by Ogero the Dane, who conquered those parts!) Cyncilim I suspect to be *Kain Kulam* or *Cai Colam*, one of the old ports a few miles north of Quilon, and the king of which is called Lingua, but his kingdom Mohebar. There is also the king of Molephatam, whose kingdom is called Molepoor, where pearls are taken in infinite quantities. There is also another king in the island of Sylen, where are found precious stones and good elephants. There be also three or four kings on the island of Java, where the good spices grow. There be also other kings, as the king of Telenc, who is very potent and great. The kingdom of Telenc abounds in corn, rice, sugar, wax, honey and honey-comb, pulse, eggs, goats, buffalos, beeves, milk, butter, and in oils of divers kinds, and in many excellent fruits, more than any other part of the Indies. There is also the kingdom of Maratha which is very great; and there is the king of Batigala, but he is of the Saracens. There be also many kings in Chopa.

42. What shall I say? The greatness of this India is beyond description. But let this much suffice concerning India the Greater and the Less.

VI.

HERE FOLLOWETH CONCERNING INDIA TERTIA.[1]

1. Of India Tertia I will say this, that I have not indeed seen its many marvels, not having been there, but have heard them from trustworthy persons. For example, there be dragons in the greatest abundance, which carry on their

formerly a little kingdom. Singuyli is not very like Kain Kulam, but Cynellim is somewhat like both; and the position in which he mentions it, between Calicut and Quilon, would suit.

As for *Chopa*, I suspect it to be a misreading (Chāpa, read as Chopa), for CHAMPA, whereby he seems to mean hazily India ultra Gangem in general, though the name belongs to Cambodia.

[2] India Tertia is apparently Eastern Africa, south of Abyssinia.

heads the lustrous stones which be called carbuncles. These animals have their lying-place upon golden sands,[1] and grow exceeding big, and cast forth from the mouth a most fetid and infectious breath, like the thickest smoke rising from fire. These animals come together at the destined time, develope wings, and begin to raise themselves in the air, and then, by the judgment of God, being too heavy, they drop into a certain river which issues from Paradise, and perish there.

2. But all the regions round about watch for the time of the dragons, and when they see that one has fallen, they wait for lxx days, and then go down and find the bare bones of the dragon, and take the carbuncle which is rooted in the top of his head, and carry it to the emperor of the Æthiopians, whom you call Prestre Johan.[2]

3. In this India Tertia are certain birds, which are called Roc, so big that they easily carry an elephant up into the air. I have seen a certain person who said that he had seen one of those birds, one wing only of which stretched to a length of eighty palms.[3]

4. In this India are the true unicorns, like a great horse, having only one horn in the forehead, very thick and sharp, but short, and quite solid, marrow and all.[4] This creature,[5]

[1] So far we have the old Herodotean myth (*Her.*, iii. 116), which Milton has rendered into stately verse—

"As when a gryphon in the wilderness
With winged course, o'er hill or moory dale,
Pursues the Arimaspian, who by stealth
Had from his wakeful custody purloined
The guarded gold"——

But the scene has been transferred from the north of Europe to Æthiopia. The rest of the fable I cannot trace.

[2] A dissertation on Prester John, and the confusions which transferred a Christian prince of Central Asia to Central Africa, will be found in M. D'Avezac's preface to *Carpini*, in the volume from which we are translating.

[3] For the Roc see *Marco*, iii. 35; *Ibn Batuta* (in *Lee*), p. 222; Sindbad the Sailor, and Aladdin! See also Mr. Major's preface to *India in the Fifteenth Century*.

[4] "*Etiam et medullâ.*"

[5] "*Istud ales*"!

it is said, is of such fierceness that it will kill an elephant, nor can it be captured except by a virgin girl. All the parts of that creature are of wonderful virtue, and the whole of them good for medicine.

5. There are other animals also of very divers species: thus, there is one like a cat, whose sweat is of such good odour that it surpasses all the other scents in the world, and that sweat is thus collected. When it sweats it rubs itself on a certain wood, and there [the sweat] becomes coagulated; then men come and collect it, and carry it away.[1]

6. Between this India and Æthiopia is said to be, towards the east, the terrestrial paradise; for from those parts come down the four rivers of Paradise, which abound exceedingly in gold and gems.

7. There be serpents with horns, and some with precious stones.[2]

8. The men of that land are very black, pot-bellied, fat, but short; having thick lips and squab nose, overhanging forehead, and hideous countenances, whilst they go altogether naked.

9. I have seen many of them. They hunt the most savage beasts, such as lions, ounces, and leopards, and most dreadful serpents; wild men they be, wild against wild beasts!

10. In this India is found embar, which is like wood, and exceeding fragrant, and is called *gemma marina*, or the Treasure of the Sea.[3]

[1] *Viverra Indica*, the civet cat, seems to be found over a great part of Asia and Africa. The perfume is secreted from very peculiar glands, existing in both sexes; and in North Africa, where the animals are kept for the purpose, the secretion is scraped from the pouch with an iron spatula, about twice a week (*Penny Cyclop.*). But the text is confirmed by Sir E. Tennent, who says that the Tamils in Northern Ceylon, who also keep the animal for its musk, collect this from the wooden bars of the cage, on which it rubs itself (*Nat. Hist. Ceylon*, p. 32).

[2] It is a Ceylonese story, according to Tennent, that the cobra's stomach sometimes contains a stone of inestimable price. The cerastes or horned adder is now well known.

[3] *Ambergris*, a substance found chiefly in warm climates, floating on the

11. There also be certain animals like an ass, but with transverse stripes of black and white, such as that one stripe is black and the next white. These animals be wonderfully beautiful.

12. Between this India and India the Greater, are said to be islands of women only, and of men only, such that the men cannot live long in the islands of the women, and *vice versa*.

13. But they can live there for some x or xv days and cohabit; and when the women produce male children they send them to the men, and when female children they retain them.[1]

14. There are many other different islands in which are men having the heads of dogs, but their women are said to be beautiful.[2] I cease not to marvel at the great variety of islands that there be.

surface of the sea or thrown on the coasts. It was formerly believed to be the exudation of a tree, but is now considered to be a morbid animal concretion, having been found in the intestinal canal of the sperm whale. It is found usually in small pieces, but some times in lumps of fifty to one hundred pounds weight. The best comes from Madagascar, Surinam, and Java. It is opaque, of a bright grey colour, softish, and when rubbed or heated exhales an agreeable odour. It is inflammable; and is used as a perfume. (*Penny Cyclop.* and *Macculloch's Commercial Dictionary.*)

[1] This strange myth is in *Marco Polo* (Part iii. c. 23). He represents the islands to be "full five hundred miles out at sea," south of Mekrán. The people of Sumatra believe that the inhabitants of Engano, a small island south of Bencoolen, are all females, and, like the mares of ancient story, are impregnated by the wind. (*Marsden's Sumatra.*)

[2] This is probably a legendary notice of the Andaman islanders, whom Polo represents as "having a head, teeth, and jaws like those of a mastiff dog" (iii. c. 16). And Ibn Batuta, describing the people of "Barah-nakár" (under which name he seems to have mixed up the stories of the Andamans which he had heard, with his experience of some port on the main at which he had touched on his way from Bengal to Sumatra), says, "Their men are of the same form with ourselves, except that their mouths are like those of dogs; *but the women have mouths like other folks*" (*Lee's Trans.*, p. 198). The stories of the Andaman islanders are as old as Ptolemy, whose *Agmatæ* (compare Polo's *Angaman*) and adjacent islands, they doubtless are. Till Dr. Mouat's account, just published, we had little more knowledge of them than these 1800-year-old legends gave us, and even now we do not know much, near as they are to Calcutta.

15. Let this suffice about India Tertia and the islands for the present.

VII.

HERE FOLLOWETH CONCERNING THE GREATER ARABIA.

1. I have been in the Greater Arabia, but can tell little, except that there grow there choice incense and myrrh.

2. The natives of this Arabia are all black, very crafty and lean, with voices like that of a little boy. They dwell in caverns and holes on the ground: they eat fish, herbs, and roots, and nothing else.[1]

3. This Arabia hath very great deserts, pathless and very dry.

4. Of Æthiopia, I say that it is a very great land, and a very hot. There are many monsters there, such as gryphons that guard the golden mountains which be there. Here, too, be serpents and other venomous beasts, of vast size and venomous exceedingly.

5. There, too, are very many pretious stones. The lord of that land I believe to be more potent than any man in the world, and richer in gold and silver and in pretious stones. He is said to have under him fifty-two kings, rich and potent. He ruleth over all his neighbours towards the south and the west.

6. In this Æthiopia are two burning mountains, and be-

[1] He had probably, during his voyages in the Persian Gulph, touched at some point of the north-east of Arabia, where Wellsted notices the peculiar wildness and low civilization of the people, "of a darker hue than the common race of Arabs;" "the greater number residing in caves and hollows;" "their principal food dates and salt fish, rice being nearly unknown to them;" whilst they testified as much surprise at the sight of looking-glasses, watches, etc., as could have been exhibited by the veriest savage of New Holland. (*Wellsted's Travels in Arabia*, i. 241-2.)

tween them a mountain of gold. The people of the country are all Christians, but heretics. I have seen and known many folk from those parts.

7. To that emperor the Soldan of Babylon giveth every year 500,000 ducats[1] of tribute as 'tis said.

8. I can tell nothing more of Æthiopia, not having been there.

VIII.

HERE FOLLOWETH CONCERNING THE GREAT TARTAR.[2]

1. Of the Great Tartar, I relate what I have heard from trustworthy persons; to wit, that he is very rich, very just, and very generous. He hath under him four realms as big as the realm of France, and well peopled too. In his dominions every person who cannot get a livelihood, may, an he will, have victual and raiment from that lord, all the days of his life.[3]

2. In his dominion is current, in place of money, paper stamped with black ink, with which can be procured gold, silver, silk, gems, and in short all that man can desire.[4]

3. In that empire are idol-temples, and also monasteries of men and women as with us; and they have a choral service and sermons just like us; and the great pontiffs of the idols wear red hats and capes like our cardinals. 'Tis incredible what splendour, what pomp, what festivity is made in the idol sacrifices.[5]

[1] "*Duplarum*."

[2] As we say in later times, "The Great Mogul".

[3] See the same statement in *Marco Polo*, i. 29.

[4] As M. Polo says, with a facetiousness unusual in him, "With regard to the money of Kambalu, the great Khan is a perfect alchymist, for he makes it himself" (i. 26).

[5] From Rubruquis to Père Huc all travellers in Buddhistic Tartary and

4. There they burn not their dead; nor do they bury them sometimes for ten years. Some defer this because they have not the means to perform the sacrifices and the obsequies as they would wish. But they keep the body in the house, and serve it with food as if it were alive.

5. The great lords, when they die, are buried with a horse, and with one or two of their best beloved slaves alive.[1]

6. In that empire are very great cities, as I have heard tell from those who have seen them; and there is one called Hyemo which it taketh a day's journey on horseback to cross, by a direct street through the middle of it.[2]

7. I have heard that that emperor hath two hundred cities under him greater than Toulouse; and I certainly believe them to have more inhabitants.

8. The folk of that empire be marvellously well-mannered, clean, courteous, and liberal withal.

9. In that empire rhubarb is found, and musk. And

Thibet have been struck by the extraordinary resemblance of many features of the ecclesiastical system and ritual to those of the Roman Church. Father Grueber, in 1661, speaking of the veneration paid to the Lama, ascribes it to "the manifest deceits of the devil, who has transferred the veneration due to the sole Vicar of Christ to the superstitious worship of barbarous nations, as he has also, in his innate malignity, parodied the other mysteries of the Christian faith." (In Kircher's *China Illustrata.*) Huc and Gabet say, "The crosier, the mitre, the dalmatica, the cope or pluvial (which the Grand Lamas wear in travelling), the double-choired liturgy, the psalmody, the exorcisms, the censer . . . the benedictions . . . the rosary, the ecclesiastical celibate, the spiritual retreats, the worship of saints; fasts, processions, holy water; in all these numerous particulars do the Buddhists coincide with us." The cardinal's red hat among the Lamas is a modern fact. (Abridged from a paper by the present writer in *Blackwood* for March 1852.)

[1] Ibn Batúta describes how at the funeral of the Great Khan four female slaves and six favourite Mamluks were buried alive with him, and four horses were impaled alive upon the tumulus; the same being done in burying his relatives, according to their degree (*Lee*, p. 220).

[2] This is perhaps the Tartar city of Iymyl, called by the Chinese Yemi-li, built by Okkodai, the son of Chengiz Khan, somewhere to the east of Lake Balkash. (See *D'Avezac's Notice of Travels in Tartary, Recueil de Voyages*, iv. p. 516). But the description rather suggests one of the vast cities of China, such as Marco Polo describes Kinsai (Hang-choo-foo).

musk is the navel of a certain wild animal like a goat, from which, when it is taken alive, the skin of the navel is cut in a round form, and the blood which flows from the wound is gathered and put into the said skin, and dried; and that makes the best musk in the world.

10. There are no other things in that empire that I am acquainted with worthy to be described, except the very beautiful and noble earthenware, full of good qualities, and [which is called] porcelain.[1]

11. When the emperor dies, he is carried by certain men with a very great treasure to a certain place, where they place the body, and run away as if the devil were after them, and others are ready incontinently to snatch up the body and bear it in like manner to another place, and so on to the place of burial; and they thus do that the place may not be found, and consequently that no one may be able to steal the treasure.[2]

12. Nor is the death of the emperor made known until another has been secretly established on the throne by his relations and the chiefs.[3]

13. That emperor bestows greater alms than any prince or lord in the world.

14. The people subject to him are for the most part idolaters.

[1] "*Vasa pulcherrima et nobilissima atque virtuosa et porseleta.*" Perhaps "full of good qualities, and of fine enamelled surface"?

[2] Carpini says that there was a certain cemetery for the emperors and chiefs, to which their bodies were carried whenever they died, and that much treasure was buried with them. No one was allowed to come near this cemetery except the keepers (*Recueil de Voyages*, iv. 631). Marco Polo says that if the chief lord died a hundred days journey from this cemetery, which was in the Altai mountains, his body must be carried thither. Also "when the bodies of the Khans are carried to these mountains, the conductors put to the sword all the men whom they meet on the road, saying, 'Go and serve the great lord in the other world;' and they do the same to the horses, killing also for that purpose the best he has" (ii. 45).

[3] This seems from Alcock to be the Japanese practice. *Le Roi est mort, vive le Roi!*

IX.

HERE FOLLOWETH CONCERNING CALDEA.

1. Of Caldea I will say not much, but yet what is greatly to be wondered at; to wit, that in a place of that country stood Babylon, now destroyed and deserted, where are hairy serpents and monstrous animals. In the same place also, in the night season, are heard such shoutings, such howlings, such hissings, that it is called Hell. There no one would dare to pass a single night, even with a great army, on account of the endless terrors and spectres.[1]

2. When I was there, there was seen a tortoise that carried five men on its back.[2]

3. Also a two-headed animal, exceeding frightful, which dared to wade across the Euphrates, and to chase the inhabitants on the other side.[3]

4. Also there be there serpents of such bulk that it is horrible to hear tell of; and I believe that that land is the habitation of demons.

[1] Doubtless our friar had in his mind the words of Isaiah, "Wild beasts of the desert shall lie there; and their houses shall be full of doleful creatures: and owls shall dwell there, and satyrs shall dance there. And the wild beasts of the island shall cry in their desolate houses, and dragons in their pleasant palaces" (xiii. 21-22).

[2] Probably a *kirbah*, or water skin, or perhaps several tied together, frequently used by the *fellahs* to cross the Tigris and Euphrates. There are no large tortoises in either of those rivers. (B.)

[3] A couple of buffalos, perhaps, which may frequently be seen swimming across the stream with only their muzzles and horns above water. (B.)

X.

HERE FOLLOWETH CONCERNING THE LAND OF ARAN.

Concerning Aran I say nothing at all, seeing that there is nothing worth noting.[1]

XI.

HERE FOLLOWETH CONCERNING THE LAND OF MOGAN.[2]

1. From the land of Mogan came three kings to worship the Lord.

2. And in a certain place there, which is called Bacu, are pits dug, whence is extracted and drawn a certain oil, which is called *naft;* and it is a very warm oil of medicinal virtue, and it burneth passing well.[3]

[1] Referring probably to Harrán, the Haran of Scripture. The country generally being desert, there was little to say about it. (B).

This chapter is a worthy parallel to that one in *Horrebow's History of Iceland,* "Concerning Owls and Snakes," which Sir Walter Scott quotes more than once with such zest.

[2] See ch. ii. parag. 7, *ante.*

[3] One of the best accounts of Baku is in the *Travels* of George Forster, of the Bengal Civil Service, who came overland from India by the Caspian in 1784. There were at that time a considerable number of Multan Hindus at Baku, where they had long been established, and were the chief merchants of Shirwán. The *Atish-gah,* or Place of Fire, was a square of about thirty yards, surrounded by a low wall, and containing many apartments, in each of which was a small jet of sulphureous fire issuing through a furnace or funnel, "constructed in the form of a Hindu altar." The fire was used for worship, cookery, and warmth. On closing the funnel the fire was extinguished, when a hollow sound was heard, accompanied by a strong and cold current of air. Exclusive of these there was a large jet from a natural cleft, and many small jets outside the wall, one of which was used by the Hindus for burning the dead.

The whole country round Baku has at times, according to Kinneir, the appearance of being enveloped in flame, and during moonlight nights in November and December a bright blue light is observed to cover the whole western range. My friend Colonel Patrick Stewart, who was lately

XII.

HERE FOLLOWETH CONCERNING THE CASPIAN HILLS.

Of the Caspian Hills I say that there they sacrifice sheep upon a cross, and they call themselves Christians, though they are not so, and know nothing of the faith.[1] Among those mountains are more than fifteen different nations.

for some days at Baku, tells me that it is often possible to "set the sea on fire", *i.e.*, the gaseous exhalations on the surface. He says the Hindus are now only two or three, one of whom, a very old man, had lost the power of speaking his native tongue.

The quantity of naphtha procured in the plain near the city is enormous. Some of the wells are computed to give from 1000 to 1500 pounds a day. It is discriminated as *black* and *white*. The white naphtha appears to be used chiefly as a remedy for allaying pains and inflammations. The flat roofs of Baku are covered with the black naphtha, and it is made into balls with sand as a fuel. (See *Forster's Journey from Bengal to England*, London, 1798; and *Macdonald Kinneir's Geog. Memoir of the Persian Empire*, p. 359.)

From Haxthausen we learn that the Átish-gáh or Âtish-jáh has been altered since Forster's time. The flame now issues from a central opening, and from four circumjacent hollow pillars within the temple, which is a building of a triangular form, and of about one hundred and ninety paces to the side, erected by a Hindu merchant in the present century. The flame is described as being about four feet high, bright, and "waving heavily to and fro against the dark sky, a truly marvellous and spectral sight." The Atish-gah of Baku appears to be the "Castle of the Fire-worshippers" spoken of by Polo (ii. 9). He says they revere the fire "as a god, and use it for burning all their sacrifices; and when at any time it goes out, they repair to that well, where the fire is never extinguished, and from it bring a fresh supply."

[1] Some trace of the practice here alluded to is to be found among the Nestorians. "Once a year there is a kind of *Agapæ* to commemorate the departed, in all the mountain villages. For days previous such families as intend to contribute to the feast are busily engaged in preparing their offerings, These consist of lambs and bread, which are brought into the church-yard; and after the people have communicated of the holy Eucharist, the priest goes forth, cuts several locks of wool off the fleeces, and throws them into a censer. Whilst a deacon swings this to and fro in presence of the assembled guests, the priest recites the following anthem:

"'THE FOLLOWING IS TO BE SAID OVER THE LAMBS THAT ARE SLAIN IN SACRIFICE FOR THE DEAD:—

. . . .

"'When ye present oblations and offer pure sacrifices, and bring lambs

XIII.

HERE FOLLOWETH CONCERNING GEORGIANA.

Of Georgiana [I have to say] that it is entirely like our country; and all the people are Christians and warriors.[1]

XIV.

HERE FOLLOWETH CONCERNING THE DISTANCES OF COUNTRIES.

1. Now I will mention in a brief statement the distances

to be slain, ye should first call the priests, who shall sign them with the sign of the cross before they are slain, and say over them these words: He was brought as a lamb to the slaughter,'" etc.

. . . . "'O Lord, let the oblation which thy servants have offered before thee this day be acceptable, as was that of faithful Abraham the righteous, who vowed his son as an oblation, and stretched out the knife upon his throat, *whereupon he saw a lamb hung on a tree like his life-giving Lord who was crucified*,'" etc. (*Rev. G. P. Badger's Nestorians*, i. 229.)

See also Dr. Stanley's account of the cruciform spit used by the Samaritans in roasting the Paschal lamb, in the notes to his *Sermons before the Prince of Wales*.

The Yezidís also have some mixture of Christian names in their superstitions, and sacrifice to Christ. Of the Ossetes of the Caucasus also we are told that the majority are nominally Christians, but in fact semi-pagans, and rarely baptized. They offer sacrifices of bread and flesh in sacred groves, and observe the Christian festivals with various sacrifices, *e.g.*, a *lamb at Easter*, a pig on New Year's Day, an ox at Michaelmas, a goat at Christmas. Both Georgians and Armenians are said still to be addicted to the practice of sacrifice in their churches. (*Haxthausen's Transcaucasia*, p. 397.)

[1] "The Georgians are the Christian, the Circassians the Mohammedan, cavaliers of the Caucasian countries; they stand in the same relative position as the Goths and Moors of Spain." "The bases and principles of the organization and general condition of the Georgian people bore great resemblance to those of the Germanic race, comprising a feudal constitution, perfectly analogous to the Romano-Germanic. In this *warlike country* the Christian hierarchy was constituted in a perfectly analogous manner to the temporal feudal state," etc. (*Haxthausen*, pp. 113, 117.)

of the countries. Know ye, then, that from this place to Constantinople 'tis about three thousand miles or more.

2. From Constantinople to Tanan[1] or Tartary is a thousand miles, going always towards the east, and by sea.

3. The empire of Persia beginneth at Trebizond, which is a city of the Greeks, situated in the furthest bight of the Moorish Sea. And that empire[2] extendeth far; for it includeth Lesser Asia, Cilicia,[3] Media, Cappadocia, Lycia, Greater Armenia, Caldea, Georgiana, part of the Caspian Hills and Mogan,—whence came those three kings to worship Christ,[4] — even to the Iron Gates,[5] and all Persia, with some part of Lesser India; so that the empire extendeth across from the Black Sea to the Indian Sea, and so great is the distance as to equal lxxxx days of ordinary journey with cattle, or more.

4. Then Lesser India extendeth four-square over LX days' journey, and is entirely level.

5. But the Greater India extendeth over more than CLXX days' journey, excluding the islands, of which there be more than XII thousand inhabited, and more than VIII thousand uninhabited, as those say who navigate that sea. And [this India also] is nearly all a plain.

6. But the vessels of these Indies be of a marvellous kind. For although they be very great, they be not put together

[1] *Tana* was the name of a place at the mouth of the Don or Tanais, the site of an early Venetian factory.

[2] See note (2) page 54.

[3] "*Cicilia*," in orig.

[4] Marco Polo also places the country of the three Magi, Balthazar, Gaspar, and Melchior, in this region (ii. 9), as appears from his connecting them with the worshipped fire at Baku. Their tombs, according to him, were in a city called Sava.

[5] The Iron Gates, at the place called by the Persians Der-bend (Dărbănd), or the Closed Gate, the capital of Daghestan, and lying in a defile between the Caucasus and the Caspian. The city is traditionally said to have been founded by Alexander, and part of the celebrated wall of Gog and Magog, said to have extended from the Black Sea to the Caspian, is to be seen here, running over high and almost inaccessible mountains. (*Kinneir's Pers. Empire*, p. 355.)

with iron, but stitched with a needle, and a thread made of a kind of grass. Nor are the vessels ever decked over, but open, and they take in water to such an extent that the men always, or almost always, must stand in a pool to bale out the water.

7. Cathay is a very great empire, which extendeth over more than C days' journey; and it hath only one lord, whereas the case with the Indies is the very opposite, for there be therein many kings, many princes, not one of whom holdeth himself tributary to another.

8. And the dominion of Æthiopia is great exceedingly; and I believe, and lie not, that the population thereof is, at the least, three times that of our Christendom.[1]

9. But other two empires of the Tartars, as I have heard, to wit, that which was formerly of Cathay, but now is of Osbet, which is called Gatzaria, and the empire of Dua and Cayda, formerly of Capac and now of Elchigaday, extend over more than CC days' journey.[2]

10. The vessels which they navigate in Cathay be very

[1] One suspects some mistake here. He would seem still to be speaking of Cathay, in which case his estimate would have some propriety.

[2] I cannot explain all these names. But the author's reference is to the several empires into which the vast conquests of Chengiz Khan were partitioned among his descendants. 1. *Cathay*, or all the eastern part of the empire, including China, with a paramount authority over all, fell to Okkodai and his successors, the "Great Khans" or "Great Tartars" of our author. 2. *Kipchak*, or Comania, all the country westward of the Ural river, through the south of Russia, fell eventually to Batu, the grandson of Chengiz, whose invasion, penetrating to Silesia and Hungary, struck terror into Europe. This is the Gatzaria of the text; Khazaria being properly the country adjoining the Sea of Azoph, and including the Crimea. The expression "now of Osbet" appears to refer to Uzbeg, who was Khan of Kipchak from 1313 to 1340. 3. *Jagatai* (Elchigaday = El Jagatai, I suppose) was Transoxiana, lying between the first and second empires. It was so called from Jagatai, the son of Chengiz, to whom it fell. *Kaidu*, the grandson of Jagatai, according to Marco Polo, was the ruler of this country in the time of that traveller. Dua and Capac I cannot explain. 4. *Persia*. The second and third are of course the "other two empires of the Tartars" mentioned in the text. (See D'Avezac's "Notice of Old Travels in Tartary in *Recueil de Voyages*, vol. iv.; and Introduction to *Erskine's Translation of Baber's Memoirs*, etc.)

big, and have upon the ship's hull more than C cabins, and with a fair wind they carry X sails, and they are very bulky, being made of three thicknesses of plank, so that the first thickness is as in our great ships, the second cross-wise, the third again long-wise. In sooth, 'tis a very strong affair.[1] It is true that they venture not far out to sea; and that Indian sea is seldom or never boisterous, and when it does rise to such a degree as they deem awfully perilous, it is such weather as our mariners here would deem splendid. For one of the men of our country would there ('tis no lie), be reckoned at sea worth a hundred of theirs and more.

11. Græcia[2] also is of great extent, but of how many days' journey I wot not.

12. One general remark I will make in conclusion; to wit, that there is no better land or fairer, no people so honest, no victuals so good and savoury, dress so handsome, or manners so noble, as here in our own Christendom; and, above all, we have the true faith, though ill it be kept. For, as God is my witness, ten times better [Christians], and more charitable withal, be those who be converted by the Preaching and Minor friars to our faith, than our own folk here, as experience hath taught me.

13. And of the conversion of those nations of India, I say this: that if there were two hundred or three hundred good friars, who would faithfully and fervently preach the Catholic faith, there is not a year which would not see more than X thousand persons converted to the Christian faith.

14. For, whilst I was among those schismatics and unbelievers, I believe that more than X thousand, or thereabouts, were converted to our faith, and because we, being few in number, could not occupy, or even visit, many parts of the

[1] See in *Ibn Batúta*, p. 172, a description of the great Chinese junks, trading at that time to Malabar. It is remarkable that the Arabian traveller uses literally the word *junk*, showing that we got it through the Arab mariners, though ultimately from the Malay *ajong*, a ship.

[2] *Sic in orig.* Qu. *Arabia?*

land, many souls (wo is me!) have perished, and exceeding many do yet perish for lack of preachers of the Word of the Lord. And 'tis grief and pain to hear how, through the preachers of the perfidious and accursed Saracens, those sects of the heathen be day by day perverted. For their preachers run about, just as we do, here, there, and everywhere over the whole Orient, in order to turn all to their own miscreance.[1] These be they who accuse us, who smite us, who cause us to be cast into durance, and who stone us; as I indeed have experienced, having been four times cast into prison by them, I mean the Saracens. But how many times I have had my hair plucked out, and been scourged, and been stoned, God himself knoweth and I, who had to bear all this for my sins, and yet have not attained to end my life as a martyr for the faith, as did four of my brethren. For what remaineth God's will be done! Nay, five Preaching Friars and four Minors were there in my time cruelly slain for the Catholic faith.

Wo is me that I was not with them there!

15. I believe moreover that the king of France might subdue the whole world to his own dominion and to the Christian faith, without the aid of any other.

XV.

HERE FOLLOWETH CONCERNING THE ISLAND OF CHIOS.

I have seen an island called Chios, where groweth mastick in very great abundance; nor do those trees when planted anywhere else in the whole world produce mastick. Mastick is the gum of a very noble tree. That island was held by a very noble Genoese, by name Martin Zachary, a most worthy

[1] It was just about this time that a great proselytizing energy was developed by Islâm in the far east, extending to Sumatra and Java.

sea captain, who slew or took more than ten thousand Turks. But, alackaday! the rascally emperor of Constantinople, Greek that he was, got possession of the island by treason, a thing most deeply to be lamented; and all the more that the captain was taken in person, and made a prisoner.

XVI.

CONCERNING TURKEY.[1]

1. I was also in Turkey, in a certain camp on the coast of the main, held by a noble Genoese, by name Andreolo Cathani, who hath with him only fifty-two knights[2] and four hundred foot soldiers. He doth much scathe to the Turks. And there he himself maketh alum, without which no cloth can be properly dyed; and 'tis made in a marvellous way, nor do I believe that the art could have been invented by human ingenuity, but rather by the Holy Spirit.[3] For thus it is: stones be taken from under the ground, not stones of any kind, but such as be specially suitable, for few be found of that kind. And these stones be baked like bricks or pottery, and that in great quantity and for many days, and with a most potent fire. The stones be afterwards placed on a great platform, and water is poured upon them, and this two or three times a day for a month continuously, so that the stones become like [slaked] lime. Afterwards they be placed in great caldrons with water, and that which falleth to the bottom is extracted with great iron ladles. Then four-square tanks of plaster are prepared, numerous and large, and into these the water from the caldrons is poured, and there gradually taketh place a precipitation like crystal, and that is choice alum.[4]

[1] *Asiatic* Turkey, of course, at this date. [2] Or horsemen.

[3] The good friar was doubtless thinking of *Exodus* xxxv. 30-31.

[4] According to Beckman, the ancients were not acquainted with real

2. In this Turkey be the VII Churches to which wrote the Blessed John in the Apocalypse, who also ordered a sepulchre to be dug for him in Ephesus, whereinto he entered and was seen no more. But I will tell one very marvellous thing concerning that excavation, as I heard it from a certain devout religious person, who was there and heard it with his own ears. From time to time is heard there a very loud sound, as of a man snoring, and yet is the sepulchre void.[1]

3. This Turkey, which is called Asia Minor, is inhabited by the Turks, and by a few schismatic Greeks and Armenians. Which Turks be most rascally Saracens, and capital archers withal, and the most warlike and perfidious of all mankind.

4. The country is very fertile, but uncultivated; for the Turks trouble not themselves.[2]

alum. He says it was discovered by the orientals, who established works in the thirteenth century in Syria (apparently at Rukka or Rochha, east of Aleppo, whence the name of *Roch-alum*, still in use). The best now comes from the neighbourhood of Civita Vecchia. The method of manufacture in England and Scotland is to mix broken alum slate with fuel, and to set it on fire. When combustion is over the residual mixture is lixiviated with water; a solution of the earthy salt being obtained, potash salts are added, and crystals of alum are the result. (*Penny Cyclop.* and *Macculloch's Comm. Dict.*)

[1] A curious instance of the persistence of legend in the face of Scripture. See *John*, xxi, 23.

[2] "*Quia Turci non multum curant.*" Some time ago a foreign ambassador at the Sublime Porte told the Grand Vizier that there were three enemies who would eventually destroy the Turkish empire, viz: *Bakalum*, (We shall see;) *In shäa-Alláh*, (If it please God;) and *Yarun sabáh* (to-morrow morning). (B.)

For this and several other very apt notes which I have marked with the letter B, I have to thank Mr. Badger's kindness.

EXPLICIT.

INDEX TO THE *MIRABILIA* OF JORDANUS AND THE COMMENTARY THEREON.

CORRIGENDA.

P. viii. *Dele* note 2, which is based on an oversight.
P. 2. Last line of note on Charybdis, insert "*which are*" after "local terms."
P. 5. Note 2, last word of second line, for "*were*" read "*was.*"
P. 12. Note 1, first line, for "*half-past nine*" read "*half-past eight.*"
P. 14. Note 1, first line, for "*Amba*" read "*Anba.*"
P. 36, § 33, first line, read "*a certain big bird like a kite.*"

THE HAKLUYT SOCIETY.

THE HAKLUYT SOCIETY, which is established for the purpose of printing rare or unpublished Voyages and Travels, aims at opening by this means an easier access to the sources of a branch of knowledge, which yields to none in importance, and is superior to most in agreeable variety. The narratives of travellers and navigators make us acquainted with the earth, its inhabitants and productions; they exhibit the growth of intercourse among mankind, with its effects on civilization, and, while instructing, they at the same time awaken attention, by recounting the toils and adventures of those who first explored unknown and distant regions.

The advantage of an Association of this kind, consists not merely in its system of literary co-operation, but also in its economy. The acquirements, taste, and discrimination of a number of individuals, who feel an interest in the same pursuit, are thus brought to act in voluntary combination, and the ordinary charges of publication are also avoided, so that the volumes produced are distributed among the Members (who can alone obtain them) at little more than the cost of printing and paper. The Society expends the whole of its funds in the preparation of works for the Members; and since the cost of each copy varies inversely as the whole number of copies printed, it is obvious that the Members are gainers individually by the prosperity of the Society, and the consequent vigour of its operations.

New Members have, at present, *the privilege of purchasing the complete set of the publications of the Society for previous years for twelve guineas, but have not the power of selecting any particular volume.*

The Members are requested to bear in mind that the power of the Council to make advantageous arrangements, will depend, in a great measure, on the prompt payment of the subscriptions, which are payable in advance on the 1st of January, and are received by MR. RICHARDS, 37, Great Queen Street, Lincoln's Inn Fields, who is the Society's agent for the delivery of its volumes. Post Office Orders should be drawn on the *Charing Cross Post Office.*

September 1863.

WORKS ALREADY ISSUED.

1—The Observations of Sir Richard Hawkins, Knt.

In his Voyage into the South Sea in 1593. Reprinted from the edition of 1622, and edited by Capt. C. R. Drinkwater Bethune, R.N., C.B. [*Issued for* 1847.

2—Select Letters of Columbus.

With Original Documents relating to the Discovery of the New World. Translated and Edited by R. H. Major, Esq., of the British Museum. [*Issued for* 1847.

3—The Discoverie of the Empire of Guiana,

By Sir Walter Ralegh, Knt. Edited, with Copious Explanatory Notes, and a Biographical Memoir, by Sir Robert H. Schomburgk, Phil. D., etc. [*Issued for* 1848.

4—Sir Francis Drake his Voyage, 1595,

By Thomas Maynarde, together with the Spanish Account of Drake's Attack on Puerto Rico, edited from the Original MSS., by W. D. Cooley, Esq. [*Issued for* 1848.

5—Narratives of Early Voyages

Undertaken for the Discovery of a Passage to Cathaia and India, by the Northwest, with Selections from the Records of the worshipful Fellowship of the Merchants of London, trading into the East Indies; and from MSS. in the Library of the British Museum, now first published, by Thomas Rundall, Esq. [*Issued for* 1849.

6—The Historie of Travaile into Virginia Britannia,

Expressing the Cosmographie and Commodities of the Country, together with the Manners and Customs of the people, gathered and observed as well by those who went first thither as collected by William Strachey, Gent., the first Secretary of the Colony; now first Edited from the original manuscript in the British Museum, by R. H. Major, Esq., of the British Museum. [*Issued for* 1849.

7—Divers Voyages touching the Discovery of America

And the Islands adjacent, collected and published by Richard Hakluyt, Prebendary of Bristol, in the year 1582. Edited, with Notes and an Introduction, by John Winter Jones, Esq., of the British Museum. [*Issued for* 1850.

8—A Collection of Documents on Japan.

With a Commentary, by Thomas Rundall, Esq. [*Issued for* 1850.

9—The Discovery and Conquest of Florida,

By Don Ferdinando de Soto. Translated out of Portuguese, by Richard Hakluyt; and Edited with Notes and an Introduction, by W. B. Rye, Esq., of the British Museum. [*Issued for* 1851.

10—Notes upon Russia,

Being a Translation from the Earliest Account of that Country, entitled Rerum Moscoviticarum Commentarii, by the Baron Sigismund von Herberstein, Ambassador from the Court of Germany to the Grand Prince Vasiley Ivanovich, in the years 1517 and 1526. Two Volumes. Translated, and Edited with Notes and an Introduction, by R. H. Major, Esq., of the British Museum. Vol. 1. [*Issued for* 1851.

11—The Geography of Hudson's Bay.

Being the Remarks of Captain W. Coats, in many Voyages to that locality, between the years 1727 and 1751. With an Appendix, containing Extracts from the Log of Capt. Middleton on his Voyage for the discovery of the North-west Passage, in H.M.S. "Furnace", in 1741-2. Edited by John Barrow, Esq., F.R.S., F.S.A. [*Issued for* 1852.

12—Notes upon Russia. Vol. 2. [*Issued for* 1852.

13—Three Voyages by the North-east,

Towards Cathay and China, undertaken by the Dutch in the years 1594, 1595, and 1596, with their Discovery of Spitzbergen, their residence of ten months in Novaya Zemlya, and their safe return in two open boats. By Gerrit de Veer. Edited by C. T. Beke, Esq., Ph.D., F.S.A. [*Issued for* 1853.

14-15—The History of the Great and Mighty Kingdom of China and the Situation Thereof.

Compiled by the Padre Juan Gonzalez de Mendoza. And now Reprinted from the Early Translation of R. Parke. Edited by Sir George T. Staunton, Bart. With an Introduction by R. H. Major, Esq. 2 vols. [*Issued for* 1854.

16—The World Encompassed by Sir Francis Drake.

Being his next Voyage to that to Nombre de Dios. Collated with an unpublished Manuscript of FRANCIS FLETCHER, Chaplain to the Expedition. With Appendices illustrative of the same Voyage, and Introduction, by W. S. W. VAUX, Esq., M.A. [*Issued for* 1855.

17—The History of the Tartar Conquerors who Subdued China.

From the French of the Père D'Orleans, 1688. Translated and Edited by the EARL OF ELLESMERE. With an Introduction by R. H. MAJOR, Esq. [*Issued for* 1855.

18—A Collection of Early Documents on Spitzbergen and Greenland,

Consisting of: a translation from the German of F. Marten's important work on Spitzbergen, now very rare; a translation from Isaac de la Peyrère's Relation de Groenland, and a rare piece entitled "God's Power and Providence showed in the miraculous preservation and deliverance of eight Englishmen, left by mischance in Greenland, anno 1630, nine moneths and twelve days, faithfully reported by Edward Pelham." Edited, with Notes, by ADAM WHITE, Esq., of the British Museum. [*Issued for* 1856.

19—The Voyage of Sir Henry Middleton to Bantam and the Maluco Islands.

From the rare Edition of 1606. Edited by BOLTON CORNEY, Esq. [*Issued for* 1856.

20—Russia at the Close of the Sixteenth Century.

Comprising "The Russe Commonwealth" by Dr. GILES FLETCHER, and SIR JEROME HORSEY'S Travels, now first printed entire from his manuscript in the British Museum. Edited by E. A. BOND, Esq., of the British Museum. [*Issued for* 1857.

21—The Travels of Girolamo Benzoni in America, in 1542-56.

Translated and edited by ADMIRAL W. H. SMYTH, F.R.S., F.S.A. [*Issued for* 1857.

22—India in the Fifteenth Century.

Being a Collection of Narratives of Voyages to India in the century preceding the Portuguese discovery of the Cape of Good Hope; from Latin, Persian, Russian, and Italian sources, now first translated into English. Edited, with an Introduction, by R. H. MAJOR, Esq., F.S.A. [*Issued for* 1858.

23—Narrative of a Voyage to the West Indies and Mexico,

In the Years 1599-1602, with Maps and Illustrations. By SAMUEL CHAMPLAIN. Translated from the original and unpublished Manuscript, with a Biographical Notice and Notes by ALICE WILMERE. Edited by NORTON SHAW. [*Issued for* 1858.

24—Expeditions into the Valley of the Amazons

During the Sixteenth and Seventeenth centuries: containing the Journey of GONZALO PIZARRO, from the Royal Commentaries of Garcilasso Inca de la Vega; the Voyage of FRANCISCO DE ORELLANA, from the General History of HERRERA; and the Voyage of CRISTOVAL DE ACUNA, from an exceedingly scarce narrative written by himself, in 1641. Edited and translated by CLEMENTS R. MARKHAM, Esq. [*Issued for* 1859.

25—Early Indications of Australia.

A Collection of Documents shewing the Early Discoveries of Australia to the time of CAPTAIN COOK. Edited by R. H. MAJOR, Esq., of the British Museum, F.S.A. [*Issued for* 1859.

26—The Embassy of Ruy Gonzalez de Clavijo to the Court of Timour, 1403-6.

Translated, for the first time, with Notes, a Preface, and an Introductory Life of Timour Beg. By CLEMENTS R. MARKHAM, Esq., F.R.G.S. [*Issued for* 1860.

27—Henry Hudson the Navigator

The Original Documents in which his career is recorded. Collected, partly Translated, and Annotated, with an Introduction, by GEORGE ASHER, Esq., LL.D. [*Issued for* 1860.

28—The Expedition of Ursua and Aguirre,

In search of El Dorado and Omagua, A.D. 1560-61, translated from the "Sexta Noticia historial" of Fray Pedro Simon, by W. BOLLAERT, Esq.; with an introduction by C. R. MARKHAM, Esq. [*Issued for* 1861.

29—The Life and Acts of Don Alonzo Enriquez de Guzman.

Translated from a Manuscript in the National Library at Madrid, and edited with Notes and an Introduction, by CLEMENTS R. MARKHAM, Esq. [*Issued for* 1862.

30—Marvels described by Friar Jordanus,

Of the Order of Preachers, native of Severac, and Bishop of Columbum; from a parchment manuscript of the Fourteenth Century, in Latin, the text of which has recently been Translated and Edited by COLONEL H. YULE, C.B., F.R.G.S., late of H.M. Bengal Engineers. [*Issued for* 1862.

31—The Travels of Ludovico di Varthema

In Syria, Arabia, Persia, India, etc., during the Sixteenth Century. Translated by J. WINTER JONES, ESQ., F.S.A., and edited, with Notes and an Introduction, by the REV. GEORGE PERCY BADGER. [*Issued for* 1863.

Other Works in Progress.

The TRAVELS OF JOSAFA BARBARO and AMBROGIO CONTARINI in Tana and Persia. Translated from Ramusio by E. A. ROY, Esq., and edited, with an Introduction, by MAJOR-GENERAL SIR HENRY RAWLINSON, K.C.B.

The TRAVELS OF PEDRO CIEZA DE LEON, from the Gulf of Darien to the city of La Plata contained in his first part of the Chronicle of Peru, which treats of the boundaries and descriptions of provinces, founding of new cities, rites and customs of the Indians and other strange things worthy to be known (Antwerp, 1554). Translated and edited, with Notes and an Introduction, by CLEMENTS R. MARKHAM, Esq., F.S.A.

The DISCOVERY AND CONQUEST OF THE CANARY ISLANDS, by BETHENCOURT in 1402-25. Translated and edited by Captain J. G. GOODENOUGH, R.N.

The Voyage of VASCO DE GAMA round the Cape of Good Hope in 1497, now first Translated from a cotemporaneous manuscript, accompanied by other documents forming a monograph on the life of DE GAMA. To be translated and edited by RICHARD GARNETT, Esq., of the British Museum.

The THREE VOYAGES OF SIR MARTIN FROBISHER, with a selection from his Letters now in the State Paper Office. Edited by Dr. RAE.

Works suggested to the Council for Publication.

The Fifth Letter of Hernando Cortes, describing his Voyage to Honduras in 1525-26.

Voyages of Alvaro de Mandana and Pedro Fernandez de Quiros in the South Seas, to be translated from Suarez de Figueroa's "Hechos del Marques da Cañete," and Torquemada's "Monarquia Indiana."

Inedited Letters, etc., of Sir Thomas Roe, during his Embassy to India.

The Travels of Friar Odoric in India.

The Voyage of John Saris to India and Japan in 1611-13, from a manuscript copy of his Journal, dated 1617.

Laws of the Hakluyt Society.

I. The object of this Society shall be to print, for distribution among its members, rare and valuable Voyages, Travels, Naval Expeditions, and other geographical records, from an early period to the beginning of the eighteenth century.

II. The Annual Subscription shall be One Guinea, payable in advance on the 1st January.

III. Each member of the Society, having paid his Subscription, shall be entitled to a copy of every work produced by the Society, and to vote at the general meetings within the period subscribed for; and if he do not signify, before the close of the year, his wish to resign, he shall be considered as a member for the succeeding year.

IV. The management of the Society's affairs shall be vested in a Council consisting of twenty-one members, viz., a President, two Vice-Presidents, a Secretary, and seventeen ordinary members, to be elected annually; but vacancies occurring between the general meetings shall be filled up by the Council.

V. A General Meeting of the Subscribers shall be held annually, on the first Thursday in March. The Secretary's Report on the condition and proceedings of the Society shall be then read, and, along with the Auditor's Report, be submitted for approval, and, finally, the Meeting shall proceed to elect the Council for the ensuing year.

VI. At each Annual Election, six of the old Council shall retire: and a list of the proposed new Council shall be printed for the subscribers previous to the general meeting.

VII. The Council shall meet ordinarily on the 2nd Monday in every month, excepting August, September, and October, for the dispatch of business, three forming a quorum, and the Chairman having a casting vote.

VIII. Gentlemen preparing and editing works for the Society, shall receive twenty-five copies of such works respectively.

IX. The number of copies printed of the Society's productions shall not exceed the estimated number of Subscribers; so that after the second year, when the Society may be supposed to have reached its full growth, there shall be no extra copies.

X. The Society shall appoint Local Secretaries, throughout the kingdom, empowered to enrol members, transmit subscriptions, and otherwise forward the Society's interests; and it shall make such arrangements with its correspondents in the chief provincial towns as will insure to subscribers residing in the country the regular delivery of their volumes at moderate charges.